READ & SPEAK
ARABIC
FOR BEGINNERS

The Easiest Way to Learn to Communicate Right Away!

Series concept
Jane Wightwick

Arabic edition
Jane Wightwick & Mahmoud Gaafar

Illustrations by
Leila Gaafar

McGraw·Hill

New York   Chicago   San Francisco   Lisbon   London   Madrid   Mexico City
Milan   New Delhi   San Juan   Seoul   Singapore   Sydney   Toronto

1 2 3 4 5 6 7 8 9 0   VLP/VLP   2 1 0 9 8 7 6 5 4 3

ISBN 0-07-143081-4 (book component)
ISBN 0-07-141215-8 (book + CD package)

McGraw-Hill books are available at special quantity discounts to use as premiums and sales promotions, or for use in corporate training programs. For more information, please write to the Director of Special Sales, Professional Publishing, McGraw-Hill, Two Penn Plaza, New York, NY 10121-2298. Or contact your local bookstore.

Other titles in this series:

Read and Speak Chinese for Beginners
Read and Speak Japanese for Beginners

Related titles:

Your First 100 Words in Arabic

This book is printed on acid-free paper.

✳ *plus...*

8 tear-out cards for fun games

Audio CD to enhance your learning

INTRODUCTION

Welcome to *Read and Speak Arabic.* This program will introduce you to the Arabic language in easy-to-follow steps. The focus is on enjoyment and understanding, on *reading* words rather than writing them yourself. Through activities and games you'll learn how to read and speak basic Arabic in less time than you thought possible.

You'll find these features in your program:

Key Words	see them written and hear them on the CD to improve your pronunciation
Language Focus	clear, simple explanations of language points to help you build up phrases for yourself
Activities	practice what you have learned in reading, listening, and speaking activities
Games	with tear-out components. Challenge yourself or play with a friend. A great, fun way to review
Audio CD	hear the key words and phrases and take part in interactive listening and speaking activities. You'll find the track numbers next to the activities in your book

If you want to give yourself extra confidence with reading the script, you will find *Your First 100 Words in Arabic* the ideal pre-course companion to this program. *Your First 100 Words in Arabic* introduces the Arabic script through 100 key everyday words, many of which also feature in *Read and Speak Arabic.*

So now you can take your first steps in Arabic with confidence, enjoyment and a real sense of progress.

Whenever you see the audio CD symbol, you'll find listening and speaking activities on your CD. The symbol shows the track number.

Track 1 is an introduction to the sounds of Arabic. Listen to this before you start and come back to it again at later stages if you need to.

Key Words

Look at the script for each key word and try to visualize it, connecting its image to the pronunciation you hear on your CD.

TRACK NUMBER 2

أهلا **ahlan**   *hello*

مع السلامة
ma'a s-salaama   *goodbye*

اسم **ism**   *name*

اسمي **ismee**   *my name*

Arabic names:

فاطمة **faaTima**[1]   *(female)*

سمير **sameer**   *(male)*

زينة **zayna**   *(female)*

يوسف **yoosef**   *(male)*

(1) Capital letters in the pronunciation, e.g. **faaTima**, indicate emphatic sounds (refer to page 91 and audio track 1).

*Remember that Arabic reads <u>right to left</u> and most short vowels (**a, i, u**) are not written as part of the main script. They can be included as marks above and below the letters but you won't normally see them. Refer to the alphabet table on page 90 if you want to work out the individual letters in a word, but try to let this happen gradually as you progress. Don't expect to take it all in at once.*

If you find yourself using strategies at first such as recognizing words by their initial letters or shapes, think of this a positive start and not as "cheating."

TOPIC 1: What's your name?

How do you say it?

Join the script to the pronunciation, as in the example.

ma'a s-salaama	أهلا
ismee	مع السلامة
yoosef	اسم
ism	اسمي
ahlan	فاطمة
faaTima	سمير
zayna	زينة
sameer	يوسف

What does it mean?

Now say the Arabic out loud and write the English next to each.
Remember to start on the *right*.

_____ مع السلامة		*hello* أهلا
_____ اسم		_____ زينة
_____ فاطمة		_____ اسمي
_____ سمير		_____ يوسف

TOPIC 1: What's your name?

Language Focus

⊙ ⊙ ⊙ ⊙ Most Arabic letters join to the next letter in a word and change their shape to a greater or lesser extent when they join. Six letters do not join, the most common of which is **alif** (ا). The table on page 90 shows how the individual letters change. As a general principle the left-hand side (or "tail") of a letter is removed before the following letter is joined.

Look at how these words you have met are formed (read <u>right to left</u>):

sameer سمير = ر + ي + م + س	**ma'a** مع = ع + م ←
zayna زينة = ة + ن + ي + ز	**ism** اسم = م + س + ا

⊙ ⊙ ⊙ ⊙ *My name* in Arabic is made up of the word اسم (**ism**) meaning *name* and the ending ـي (**-ee**) meaning *my*. Notice when you join the ending, the tail of the م is taken off: اسمي (**ismee**).

⊙ ⊙ ⊙ There is no equivalent of *is*, so to make a sentence all you have to do is to add your own name:

> اسمي فاطمة. **ismee faaTima.** *My name is Fatima.*

⊙ ⊙ It is also common to add أنا **ana** (*I*) in front of اسمي **ismee** (*my name*):

> أنا اسمي سمير. **ana ismee sameer.** *My name is Sameer.*

⊙ When you address someone you already know by their name, you can put يا (**yaa**) in front of their name:

> أهلا يا زينة. **ahlan yaa zayna.** *Hello, Zayna.*
> أهلا يا يوسف. **ahlan yaa yoosef.** *Hello, Yoosef.*

⊙
⊙ *Practice introducing yourself and learn some*
⊙ *useful replies on your CD.*
⊙

TRACK NUMBER
3

TOPIC 1: What's your name?

What are they saying?

Write the correct number in the word balloons.

1 أهلا، أنا اسمي فاطمة.
ahlan, ana ismee faaTima.

2 أهلا يا سمير.
ahlan yaa sameer.

3 مع السلامة!
ma'a s-salaama.

4 أهلا يا زينة
ahlan yaa zayna.

What do you hear?

Work out the phrases below. Then listen and check (✔) the two phrases you hear on your audio CD.

TRACK NUMBER
4

1 مع السلامة يا فاطمة! ☐   **4** أهلا يا زينة. ☐

2 أنا اسمي سمير. ☐   **5** أهلا! ☐

3 مع السلامة يا يوسف! ☐

TOPIC 1: What's your name?

Key Words

ما؟ **maa?** — *what (is)?*

اسمك **ismak** (feminine: **ismik**) — *your name*

من فضلك **min faDlak** (feminine: **min faDlik**) — *please*

شكرا **shukran** — *thank you*

صباح **SabaaH** — *morning*

مساء **masaa'** — *evening*

صباح الخير **sabaaH al-khayr** — *good morning*

مساء الخير **masaa' al-khayr** — *good evening*

Language Focus

You already know how to say *name* – اسم (ism) and <u>*my name*</u> – اسمي (ism<u>ee</u>). To say <u>*your*</u> *name* you need to add the ending ك : اسمك (ismak). The pronunciation changes to ism<u>ik</u> when referring to a female, but the Arabic spelling remains the same. The same is true with the phrase من فضلك *please*, which literally means "from your favor," and is pronounced **min faDlak** when talking to a male, but **min faDlik** when talking to a female.

To ask someone their name, add *what* ما (maa) in front of اسمك (ismak/ismik):

ما اسمك؟ **maa ismak?**
What's your name? (to a male)

ما اسمك؟ **maa ismik?**
What's your name? (to a female)

اسمي سمير. **ismee sameer.**
My name's Sameer.

أنا اسمي فاطمة. **ana smee faaTima.** *My name's Fatima.*

TOPIC 1: What's your name?

ACTIVITIES

At the conference

TRACK NUMBER 6

You are registering your name at a conference.
Take part in the conversation on your CD with the receptionist.

What does it mean?

Match the English word balloons to the Arabic.
For example: **1d**

1	Good morning.
2	Hello.
3	What's your name?
4	Please.
5	My name's Fatima.
6	Thank you.

a	من فضلك.
b	أنا اسمي فاطمة.
c	شكرا.
d	صباح الخير.
e	ما اسمك؟
f	أهلا.

Which word?

Write the correct number of the word in the box to
complete the conversation, as in the example.
(Don't forget, read right to left.)

_____ 2 _____ الخير.

أهلا. مساء _____.

أنا _____ يوسف. _____ اسمك؟

اسمي _____.

| 1 اسمي | 2 مساء |
| 3 ما | 4 زينة | 5 الخير |

TOPIC 1: What's your name?

Language Focus

○ ○ ○ ○ ○ ○ The most common way of saying *Mr.* is using الأستاذ (**al-ustaatн**) in front of either the first or the second name: الأستاذ علي (**al-ustaatн 'alee**); الأستاذ الحلبي (**al-ustaatн al-Halabee**). *Mrs.* or *Ms.* is most commonly مدام (**madaam**): مدام زينة (**madaam zayna**); مدام الحلبي (**madaam al-Halabee**). *Miss* is الآنسة (**al-aanisa**), usually used with the first name: الآنسة فاطمة (**al-aanisa faaTima**).

○ ○ ○ ○ English names with an Arabic pronunciation twist can sound a bit different. Vowels tend to be written long to distinguish them from Arabic words, so *Harry* becomes **haari** (هاري). Arabic also doesn't have the sound "*p*," so "*b*" is usually substituted: *Peter* becomes **beetar** (بيتر) and *Penny* becomes **bini** (بني). Consonant clusters (groups of consonants together) are alien to the Arab ear, turning names like *Charles* into **tishaarliz** (تشارلز).

What are their names?

Can you work out these English names written in Arabic script?
Use the alphabet table on page 90 to help you if you want.

	جاين	___Suzanne___	سوزان
_____	نانسي	_____	توني
_____	مارك	_____	لوسي
_____	ماري	_____	سام

In or out?

Who is in the office today and who is out at meetings? Look at the wallchart and write the names in English in the correct column, as in the example.

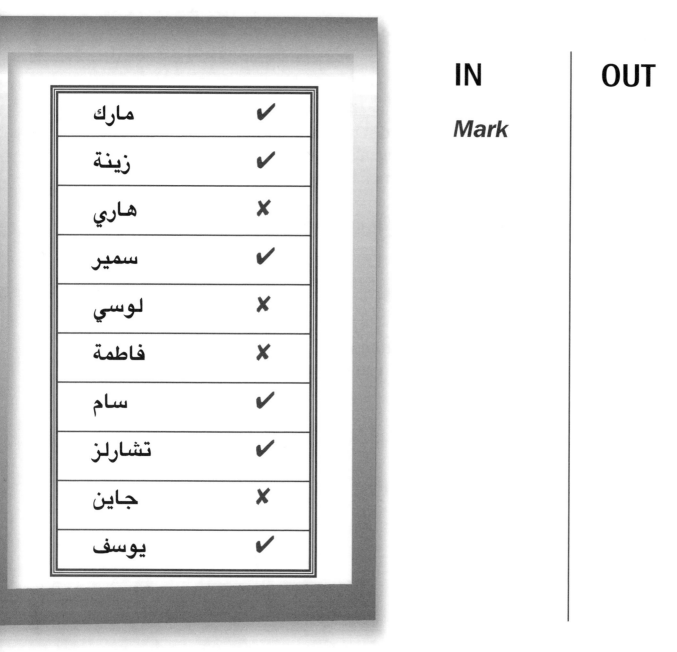

مارك	✔
زينة	✔
هاري	✘
سمير	✔
لوسي	✘
فاطمة	✘
سام	✔
تشارلز	✔
جاين	✘
يوسف	✔

IN

Mark

OUT

TOPIC 1: What's your name?

The Name Game

1. Tear out Game Card 1 at the back of your book and cut out the name cards (leave the sentence-build cards at the bottom of the sheet for the moment).

2. Put the cards Arabic side up and see if you can recognize the names. Turn over the cards to see if you were correct.

3. Keep shuffling the cards and testing yourself until you can read all the names.

4. Then cut out the extra sentence-build cards at the bottom of the sheet and make mini-dialogs. For example:

– sabaaH al-khayr. maa ismak?

– ahlan. ismee sameer.

5. You can also play with a friend. Make mini-dialogs for each other to read. If you both have a book, you can play Pairs (pelmanism) with both sets of sentence-build cards, saying the words as you turn over the cards.

GAME CARD ❶ (see page 13)

Name cards:

سمير	يوسف	زينة	فاطمة
تشارلز	بيتار	هاري	فرايا
مارك	نانسي	جاين	سام
لوسي	توني	سوزان	باني

Sentence build cards:

؟	اسمي	الأستاذ	صباح
	الأنسة	شكرا	الخير
يا	اسمك	من فضلك	مساء
ما	الأستاذة	مع سلامة	أهلا

TOPIC 1: What's your name?

Key Words

مصر **miSr**	*Egypt*	
العراق **al-'iraaq**	*Iraq*	
سوريا **sooriya**	*Syria*	
أمريكا **amreeka**	*America*	
بلد **balad**	*country*	

بريطانيا **biriTaanya**	*Britain*	
كندا **kanada**	*Canada*	
إيرلندا **eerlanda**	*Ireland*	
أستراليا **usturalya**	*Australia*	
مدينة **madeena**	*city*	

TRACK NUMBER
7

Notice that when an Arabic word starts with a vowel, this is written with an **alif** (ا), often with a small symbol called a **hamza** above (أ), or below (إ) if the word starts with **i** or **ee**.

To learn new words, try covering the English and looking at the Arabic script and pronunciation. Start from the first word and work your way to the last word seeing if you can remember the English. Then do the same but this time starting from the bottom and moving up to the first word. See if you can go down and up three times without making any mistakes. Then try looking only at the Arabic script. When you can recognize all the words, cover the Arabic and this time look at the English saying the Arabic out loud.

TOPIC 2: Where are you from?

Where are the countries?

Write the number next to the country, as in the example.

أمريكا _2_   إيرلندا ____   أستراليا ____   مصر ____

العراق ____   سوريا ____   بريطانيا ____   كندا ____

How do you say it?

Join the English to the pronunciation and the Arabic script, as in the example.

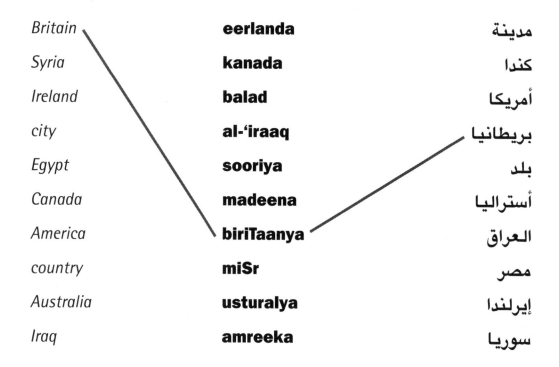

Britain	eerlanda	مدينة
Syria	kanada	كندا
Ireland	balad	أمريكا
city	al-'iraaq	بريطانيا
Egypt	sooriya	بلد
Canada	madeena	أستراليا
America	biriTaanya	العراق
country	miSr	مصر
Australia	usturalya	إيرلندا
Iraq	amreeka	سوريا

Where are the cities?

Now look at these cities and make sentences, using the word فی **fee** (in), for example:

دمشق فی سوریا. **dimashq fee sooriya.** *Damascus (is) in Syria.*

New York	*Cairo*	*London*	*Damascus*
نیو یورك	القاهرة	لندن	دمشق
nyoo yoork	**al-qaahira**	**lundun**	**dimashq**

Sydney	*Washington*	*Toronto*	*Dublin*
سيدني	واشنطن	تورنتو	دبلن
sidnee	**waashinTun**	**torunto**	**dublin**

TOPIC 2: Where are you from?

Language Focus

◉ ◉ ◉ ◉ ◉ It is straightforward to say where you're from. Use the phrase أنا من **ana min** (*I [am] from*) and add the name of the country or town:

> أنا من سوريا. **ana min sooriya.** *I'm from Syria.*
>
> أنا من أمريكا. **ana min amreeka.** *I'm from America.*
>
> أنا من القاهرة. **ana min al-qaahira.** *I'm from Cairo.*

◉ ◉ ◉ ◉ You could use في **fee** (*in*) or قريبة من **qareeba min** (*near to*) to be more specific:

> أنا من دمشق في سوريا. **ana min dimashq fee sooriya.**
> *I'm from Damascus in Syria.*
>
> أنا من أكسفورد، مدينة قريبة من لندن. **ana min oksfoord,**
> **madeena qareeba min lundun.** *I'm from Oxford, a city near London.*

◉ ◉ ◉ If you want to ask someone where they are from, you need to use the question أنت من أين؟ **anta min ayna?** (*"you from where?"*). The pronunciation of *"you"* changes slightly if you are asking a female: **anti min ayna?** The basic spelling is the same, with the only difference being in the vowel markings (see page 90).

> أنت من أين يا يوسف؟ **anta min ayna yaa yoosef?**
> *Where are you from, Yoosef?*
>
> أنت من أين يا زينة؟ **anti min ayna yaa zayna?**
> *Where are you from, Zayna?*

TRACK NUMBER
8

◉ *Listen to these six people introducing themselves and see if*
◉ *you can understand where they are from: Yoosef, Lucy,*
◉ *Sameer, Harry, Fatima, Suzanne.*

TOPIC 2: Where are you from?

Where are they from?

Join the people to the places they are from, as in the example.
Listen again to track 8 on your CD if you need to remind yourself.

دمشق	لوسي
أكسفورد	فاطمة
تورنتو	سمير
برينستون	يوسف
بغداد	سوزان
القاهرة	هاري

Where are you from?

TRACK NUMBER
9

Now say where you're from.
Follow the prompts on your audio CD.

Key Words

TRACK NUMBER
10

أنا **ana**	I	هي **hiya**	she
أنت **anta/anti**	you	من **min**	from
هو **huwa**	he	أين؟ **ayna?**	where?

TOPIC 2: Where are you from?

Language Focus

◎ ◎ ◎ ◎ ◎ You now know how to ask and answer questions about where you're from:

> أنت من أين؟ **anta/anti min ayna?** *Where are you from?*
>
> أنا من إيرلندا. **ana min eerlanda.** *I'm from Ireland.*

◎ ◎ ◎ ◎ If you want to talk about where someone else is from, you can use
هو **huwa** (*he*) or هي **hiya** (*she*):

> هو من أين؟ **huwa min ayna?** *Where's he from?*
>
> هو من أمريكا. **huwa min amreeka.** *He's from America.*
>
> هي من أين؟ **hiya min ayna?** *Where's she from?*
>
> هي من دمشق في سوريا. **hiya min dimashq fee sooriya.**
> *She's from Damascus in Syria.*

◎ ◎ ◎ You may have noticed that some countries and cites start with الـ **al-**,
meaning *the*: العراق **al-'iraaq** (*Iraq*); القاهرة **al-qaahira** (*Cairo*).

◎ ◎ You will learn more about **al-** in later topics. For the moment you need to
know that when **al-** follows في **fee** (*in*), the combination is pronounced **fil**:

> هو من بغداد في العراق. **huwa min baghdaad fil-'iraaq.**
> *He's from Baghdad in Iraq.*

TOPIC 2: Where are you from?

Who's from where?

Make questions and answers about where these people are from.
Try to include a city that you know in the answer, as in the example.

هو من أين؟

huwa min ayna?

Where's he from?

هو من نيو يورك في أمريكا.

huwa min nyoo yoork fee amreeka.

He's from New York in America.

TOPIC 2: Where are you from?

Listen and check

Listen to the conversation on your audio CD and decide if these sentences are true or false.

	True	False
1 The conversation takes place in the morning.	☐	☐
2 The woman's name is Sophie.	☐	☐
3 She comes from Canada.	☐	☐
4 The man's name is Munir.	☐	☐
5 He comes from Egypt.	☐	☐
6 They are already friends.	☐	☐

What does it mean?

Now read the Arabic you heard in the conversation and match it with English, as in the example.

What does it mean?

Read these sentences out loud and write the English next to each.

ــــــــــــــــــــــــــــ اسمي زينة.	_My name's Louise._ اسمي لويز.
ــــــــــــــــــــــــــــ هو من أين؟	ــــــــــــــــــــــــــــ أنا من كندا.
ــــــــــــــــــــــــــــ هو من لندن.	ــــــــــــــــــــــــــــ منير من مصر.
ــــــــــــــــــــــــــــ هي من أمريكا.	ــــــــــــــــــــــــــــ ما اسمك؟

Now complete this description of yourself. Read the sentences out loud, adding your own details.

.(country) في (city/town) أنا من .(name) اسمي ←

Key Words

	لبنان lubnaan	Lebanon		تونس toonis	Tunisia
	المغرب al-maghrib	Morocco		الجزائر al-jazaa'ir	Algeria
	الكويت al-kuwait	Kuwait		السعودية as-sa'oodiyya	Saudi

> There are more than 20 Arabic-speaking countries, spread throughout North Africa and Asia. Here are six more Arab nations with their flags. You'll need these to play the game.

TOPIC 2: Where are you from?

The Flag Game

① Tear out Game Card 2.

② Find a die and counter(s).

③ Put the counter(s) on START.

④ Throw the die and move that number of squares.

⑤ When you land on a flag, you must ask and answer the appropriate question for that country. For example:

أنت من أين؟ **anta (anti) min ayna?**
(*Where are you from?*)
أنا من بريطانيا. **ana min biriTaanya.**
(*I'm from Britain.*)

⑥ If you can't remember the question or answer, you must go back to the square you came from. You must throw the exact number to finish.

⑦ You can challenge yourself or play with a friend.

Key Words

كرسي **kursee** — chair

مائدة **maa'ida** — table

تليفزيون **tileefizyoon** — television

كتاب **kitaab** — book

حقيبة **Haqeeba** — bag

كمبيوتر **kumbiyootir** — computer

باب **baab** — door

شباك **shubbaak** — window

قلم **qalam** — pen

مجلة **majalla** — magazine

كنبة **kanaba** — sofa

تليفون **tileefoon** — telephone

Listen first to the key words on your CD. Then look around the room you're in and try to use the words to name as many objects as you can find. Count how many Arabic words you use.

Then look back at the list and review the words you couldn't remember. Try again to name objects and see if you can beat your first score.

What does it mean?

Match the Arabic with the pictures, then write the pronunciation and the English, as in the example.

قلم _____

كنبة _____

حقيبة _____

كمبيوتر _____

شباك *shubbaak (window)* _____

باب _____

مائدة _____

كرسي _____

تليفزيون _____

مجلة _____

تليفون _____

كتاب _____

Read & Speak ARABIC 26

ACTIVITIES

Word Square

Can you find the 8 key words in the word square?
Circle them and write the English, as in the example.

ج	بـ	ـشـ	ـة	بـ	يـ	ق	حـ
ب	ـا	ـت	كـ	جـ	و	غـ	ـل
م	ـة	بـ	ـنـ	كـ	عـ	ز	ظ
ي	جـ	يـ	م	ـل	قـ	ا	ذ
ع	ـتـ	جـ	ـل	سـ	م	ا	ت
ث	ز	بـ	كـ	ا	بـ	ـشـ	ضـ
ن	و	ـفـ	يـ	ـل	ـتـ	م	و
ي	سـ	ر	كـ	ـنـ	ب	ا	بـ

bag _____

_____

_____

_____

_____

_____

_____

_____

Odd One Out

Which is the odd one out? Circle the word that doesn't belong in each row.

سمير * سوزان * تليفزيون * فاطمة

مائدة * كرسي * باب * اسم

مجلة * كتاب * قلم * مساء

مصر * تليفون * أمريكا * العراق

صباح الخير * كنبة * أهلا * مع السلامة

Language Focus

◎ ◎ ◎ ◎ ◎ Arabic nouns (naming words) are either *masculine* (هو **huwa** *he*) or *feminine* (هي **hiya** *she*). There is no equivalent of the English *it*. Nearly all feminine nouns either end in a special feminine ending **-a** (ة) known as **taa marbooTa**, or are words which refer to female people (or both). You can assume a word is masculine unless it falls into one of these two categories.

masculine nouns	*feminine nouns*
يوسف (**yoosef** *Yoosef*)	زينة (**zayna** *Zayna*)
اسم (**ism** *name*)	مجلة (**majalla** *magazine*)
كتاب (**kitaab** *book*)	مائدة (**maa'ida** *table*)
ولد (**walad** *boy*)	بنت (**bint** *girl*)

◎ ◎ ◎ ◎ *This* in Arabic is هذا **haатна** for masculine nouns and هذه **haатнihi** for feminine nouns. There is no equivalent of the English *a/an* or *is*, so you can make simple sentences using *this* + noun:

هذا كتاب. **haатна kitaab.** *This (is a) book.*

هذه مجلة. **haатнihi majalla.** *This (is a) magazine.*

◎ ◎ ◎ Use ما **maa** (*what?*) and هل **hal** (a general question marker) to make questions. *No* is لا **laa** and *yes* is نعم **na'm**.

ما هذا؟ هذا قلم. **maa haатна? haатна qalam.**
What's this? It's a pen.

هل هذه مجلة؟. **hal haатнihi majalla?** *Is this a magazine?*

نعم، هي مجلة./لا، هو كتاب. **na'm, hiya majalla./**
laa, huwa kitaab. *Yes, it's a magazine./No, it's a book*

Ask and answer the questions. Follow the prompts on your CD.

TRACK NUMBER
14

What's this?

Look at the pictures of everyday objects from unusual angles. Then read the sentences and decide which picture they describe, as in the example.

5 هذا باب. ــــــ

1 هذا كرسي. __e__

6 هذا تليفزيون. ــــــ

2 هذا كمبيوتر. ــــــ

7 هذا قلم. ــــــ

3 هذه كنبة. ــــــ

8 هذه حقيبة. ــــــ

4 هذا تليفون. ــــــ

Key Words

شاي **shaay**	*tea*	كعكة **ka'ka**	*cake*
قهوة **qahwa**	*coffee*	فلافل **falaafil**	*falafel*
سندويتش **sandawitsh**	*sandwich*	فطيرة **faTeera**	*pancake*

Language Focus

◎ ◎ ◎ ◎ ◎ The easiest way to ask for something in a café or store is to use the phrase ممكن ...؟ **mumkin ...?** (approximately meaning *possible ...?*), or the more formal phrase أريد ... **ureed ...** (*I'd like ...*), and add *please*: من فضلك **min faDlak** (**min faDlik** when talking to a woman).

◎ ◎ ◎ ◎ Use و **wa** (*and*) to ask for more than one thing. Notice that و **wa** is written next to the following word without a space in Arabic script:

> ممكن شاي من فضلك؟ **mumkin shaay min faDlak?**
> *May I have a tea, please?*
>
> أريد قهوة وفطيرة من فضلك. **ureed qahwa wa-faTeera min faDlak.** *I'd like a coffee and a pancake, please.*

◎ ◎ ◎ *Here you are* is تفضل **tafaDDal** to a man or تفضلي **tafaDDalee** to a woman.

> ممكن سندويتش من فضلك؟ **mumkin sandwitsh min faDlak?**
> *May I have a sandwich, please?*
>
> تفضلي يا مدام. **tafaDDalee yaa madaam.**
> *Here you are, madam.*

Who orders what?

TRACK NUMBER
16

What are the customers ordering? Listen to your CD and check what they order, as in the example.

	tea	coffee	sandwich	cake	falafel	pancake
Customer 1		✓			✓	
Customer 2						
Customer 3						
Customer 4						
Customer 5						

Now look at the table and pretend you are ordering for yourself. Try to use the two ways you know of asking for something:

mumkin qahwa wa-falaafil min faDlak? ممكن قهوة وفلافل من فضلك؟

ureed qahwa wa-falaafil min faDlak. أريد قهوة وفلافل من فضلك.

TOPIC 3: What's this?

Unscramble the conversation

Can you put this conversation in the correct order?

صباح الخير. أريد قهوة من فضلك. b
SabaaH al-khayr. ureed qahwa min faDlak.

شكرا. a
shukran

تفضل. قهوة وفطيرة. d
tafaDDal. qahwa wa-faTeera.

نعم... وما هذا؟ c
na'm... wa-maa haatнa?

هذه فطيرة. f
haatнihi faTeera.

قهوة؟ e
qahwa?

ممكن فطيرة من فضلك؟ h
mumkin faTeera min faDlak?

صباح الخير. g
SabaaH al-khayr.

ORDER: g, _____

Now check your answer with the conversation on your audio CD.

TRACK NUMBER
17

TOPIC 3: What's this?

At the café

Your turn to order now. Look at the menu below and then you'll be ready to order from the waiter on your CD.

Did you work out what the café is called? Yes, it's Ali Baba (علي بابا) !

The Café Game

1. Cut out the picture cards from Game Card 3.

2. Put the cards into a bag.

3. Shake the bag.

4. Pull out a card without looking.

5. Ask for the item on the card. For example:
   mumkin shaay min faDlak? ممكن شاي من فضلك؟
   (*Can I have [a] tea, please?*)

6. If you can ask the question out loud quickly and fluently, then put the card aside. If not, then put it back into the bag.

7. See how long it takes you to get all of the cards out of the bag. Or play with a friend and see who can collect the most cards.

Key Words

غرفة **ghurfa**	*room*	بيت **bayt**	*house*
ثلاجة **thallaaja**	*refrigerator*	شجر **shajar**	*trees*
ستار **sitaar**	*curtains*	سيارة **sayyaara**	*car*
فرن **furn**	*stove*	قطة **qiTTa**	*cat*
سرير **sareer**	*bed*	كلب **kalb**	*dog*
صورة **Soora**	*picture*	فأر **faar**	*mouse*

Language Focus

⊙ ⊙ ⊙ ⊙ ⊙ Although Arabic does not have an equivalent of *a/an*, it does have an equivalent of *the*: الــ.... **al-**. The word الــ.... **al-** is written joined to the noun it refers to:

كلب **kalb** *(a) dog*	الكلب **al-kalb**	*the dog*
غرفة **ghurfa** *(a) room*	الغرفة **al-ghurfa**	*the room*

⊙ ⊙ ⊙ ⊙ With approximately half the letters of the Arabic alphabet the "l" sound of **al** is assimilated ("taken over") by the sound of the first letter of the following word. These letters are called *sun letters*. Try to recognize this assimilation but don't worry too much as you will be understood if you pronounce the "l."

سيارة **sayyaara** *(a) car*	السيارة **as-sayyaara**	*the car*
صورة **Soora** *(a) picture*	الصورة **aS-Soora**	*the picture*

TOPIC 4: Where is it?

What does it mean?

Join the Arabic to the pronunciation and write down what they mean in English.

_____	**sareer**	فرن
_____	**bayt**	كلب
_____	**kalb**	غرفة
_____	**sitaar**	قطة
stove	**furn**	سرير
_____	**ghurfa**	صورة
_____	**Soora**	ثلاجة
_____	**shajar**	شجر
_____	**sayyaara**	بيت
_____	**qiTTa**	سيارة
_____	**thallaaja**	فأر
_____	**faar**	ستار

What can you see?

Look at the picture and check (✔) the things you can see, as in the example.

☐ كلب	☑ قطة
☐ ستار	☐ شباك
☐ شجر	☐ فرن
☐ سرير	☐ باب
☐ صورة	☐ حقيبة
☐ ثلاجة	☐ تليفزيون
☐ كتاب	☐ كمبيوتر
☐ سيارة	☐ قلم
☐ تليفون	☐ مجلة
☐ مائدة	☐ كرسي

Key Words

TRACK NUMBER
20

في **fee** *in*

على **'ala** *on*

تحت **taHt** *under*

فوق **fawq** *above*

أمام **amaam**
in front of

وراء **waraa**
behind

بجانب **bi-jaanib**
next to

Language Focus

⊙ ⊙ ⊙ ⊙ ⊙ When ...الـ **al-** (*the*) is preceded by a word which ends with a vowel, the **a** of **al-** is dropped. The spelling is not affected.

الغرفة **al-ghurfa** *the room* → في الغرفة **fi l-ghurfa** *in the room*

الكرسي **al-kursee** *the chair* → على الكرسي **ala l-kursee** *on the chair*

TRACK NUMBER
21

⊙ *Practice saying where things are on your CD.*

TOPIC 4: Where is it?

Which word?

Put a circle around the word
that correctly describes each
picture, as in the example.

1 السيارة (أمام) البيت.
في

2 التليفزيون فوق الشباك.
تحت

3 الصورة أمام الكنبة.
فوق

4 الكمبيوتر على المائدة.
بجانب

5 الثلاجة فوق الفرن.
بجانب

6 الكلب تحت الكرسي.
وراء

7 البنت وراء الباب.
تحت

8 الكلب أمام السيارة.
في

Language Focus

A useful Arabic phrase when describing places is هناك (**hunaaka**), which is the equivalent of the English *there is* or *there are*.

Arabic doesn't use *is* or *are*, so this phrase doesn't change depending on whether you are talking about one thing (*singular*) or more than one thing (*plural*). You simply use هناك (**hunaaka**) followed by the noun:

> **hunaaka bank.** *There is a bank.* هناك بنك.
>
> **hunaaka shajar.** *There are trees .* هناك شجر.

In this way you can make simple descriptions using the positional words and vocabulary you have already met in this book:

> **hunaaka bank fil-madeena.** هناك بنك في المدينة.
> *There is a bank in the town.*
>
> **hunaaka shajar bi-jaanib il-bayt.** هناك شجر بجانب البيت.
> *There are trees next to the house.*

If you want to ask a question, simply add the question marker هل (**hal**) at the beginning:

> **hal hunaaka bank fil-madeena?** هل هناك بنك في المدينة؟
> *Is there a bank in the town?*
>
> **hal hunaaka shajar?** هل هناك شجر؟
> *Are there [any] trees?*

> *Look around the room you are in at the moment, or think of a room you know well. Can you describe where some of the things are using هناك?*

TOPIC 4: Where is it?

Where are the mice?

See how many mice you can find in the picture and make sentences about them using the sentence table, as in the example.

Example:

هناك فأر أمام السرير.

There's a mouse in front of the bed.

الفرن.	في ...	هناك فأر ...
الكمبيوتر.	على ...	
التليفزيون.	فوق ...	
الكرسي.	تحت ...	
الكنبة.	بجانب ...	
السرير.	أمام ...	
المائدة.	وراء ...	
الثلاجة.		

Language Focus

⊙ ⊙ ⊙ ⊙ ⊙ The most common regular Arabic plural is the ending ات -**aat**. The words below from topics 3 and 4 can be made plural using ات -**aat**. Notice that if the singular ends with the feminine -a (ة), you must remove this before adding ات -**aat**.

	singular	plural
television	تليفزيون **tileefizyoon**	تليفزيونات **tileefizyoonaat**
computer	كمبيوتر **kumbiyoortir**	كمبيوترات **kumbiyoortiraat**
magazine	مجلة **majalla**	مجلات **majallaat**
telephone	تليفون **tileefoon**	تليفونات **tileefoonaat**
refrigerator	ثلاجة **thallaaja**	ثلاجات **thallaajaat**
car	سيارة **sayyaara**	سيارات **sayyaaraat**

⊙ ⊙ ⊙ ⊙ However, many Arabic plurals are irregular, similar to the English *man/men* or *mouse/mice*. As a beginner, you'll need to learn these plurals individually. Later, patterns will emerge that will help you. From now on we will add useful plurals in brackets in the key words panels. Here are the other words you already know with their plurals:

	singular	plural
chair	كرسي **kursee**	كراسي **karaasee**
table	مائدة **maa-ida**	موائد **mawaa-id**
book	كتاب **kitaab**	كتب **kutub**
bag	حقيبة **Haqeeba**	حقائب **Haqaa-ib**
door	باب **baab**	أبواب **abwaab**
window	شباك **shubbaak**	شبابيك **shabaabeek**
pen	قلم **qalam**	أقلام **aqlaam**
room	غرفة **ghurfa**	غرف **ghuraf**
cutains	ستار **sitaar**	ستائر **sataa'ir**
stove	فرن **furn**	أفران **afraan**
bed	سرير **sareer**	أسرة **asirra**
picture	صورة **Soora**	صور **Suwar**
house	بيت **bayt**	بيوت **buyoot**
tree	شجرة **shajara**	شجر **shajar**
cat	قطة **qiTTa**	قطط **qiTaT**
dog	كلب **kalb**	كلاب **kilaab**
mouse	فأر **faar**	فئران **fi'raan**

TOPIC 4: Where is it?

◎ ◎ ◎ The opposite of هناك **hunaaka** (*there is/are*) is ليس هناك
laysa hunaaka (*there isn't/aren't*):

هناك سيارات أمام البيت. **hunaaka sayyaaraat amaam il-bayt.**
There are cars in front of the house.

ليس هناك سيارات أمام البيت. **laysa hunaaka sayyaaraat
amaam il-bayt.** *There aren't any cars in front of the house.*

Listen and learn

TRACK NUMBER
22

You'll find an activity on your CD to
help you remember the plurals.

True or False?

Decide if the sentences describing
the picture are true or false.

	True	False
1 هناك ثلاجة في الغرفة.	☑	☐
2 هناك كلب تحت المائدة.	☐	☐
3 الفرن بجانب الثلاجة.	☐	☐
4 هناك شجر وراء الثلاجة.	☐	☐
5 ليس هناك فأر تحت المائدة.	☐	☐
6 هناك شباك في الغرفة.	☐	☐
7 ليس هناك ستائر على الشباك.	☐	☐
8 التليفون على الفرن.	☐	☐
9 هناك سرير في الغرفة.	☐	☐
10 ليس هناك تليفزيون في الغرفة.	☐	☐

TOPIC 4: Where is it?

Language Review

You're half way through this program – congratulations! This is a good time to summarize the main language points covered so far in *Read and Speak Arabic*.

1 Arabic has two genders: *masculine* and *feminine*. Nearly all feminine words either end in ة **-a** (e.g. غرفة **ghurfa** *room*) or refer to female people (e.g. بنت **bint** *girl*).

2 الـ **al-** means *the*. There is no equivalent of *a/an*. Certain letters of the alphabet assimilate the "l" sound of **al-**. The "a" of **al-** is dropped when preceded by a vowel. These changes affect only the pronunciation, not the spelling.

قلم **qalam** (a) pen	القلم **al-qalam** the pen
صور **Suwar** pictures	الصور **aS-Suwar** the pictures
حقيبة **Haqeeba** (a) bag	في الحقيبة **fi l-Haqeeba** in the bag

3 You can ask for something by using the phrase ممكن... **mumkin...** or أريد... **ureed...**, but من فضلك **min faDlak** is fairly essential either way.

4 The verb *to be* (*am/is/are*) is not generally used in the present. Simple sentences and questions can be formed without the verb *to be*:

اسمي سمير.	**ismee sameer.**	*My name (is) Sameer.*
أنا من العراق.	**ana min al-'iraaq.**	*I (am) from Iraq.*
هذا قلم.	**haaтнa qalam.**	*This (is a) pen.*
هو من أين؟	**huwa min ayna?**	*Where (is) he from?*
هل القلم تحت السرير؟	**hal al-qalam taHt as-sareer?**	
(Is) the pen under the bed?		
هناك كلاب في البيت.	**hunaaka kilaab fil-bayt.**	
There (are) dogs in the house.		

5 The most common *regular* plural ending is ـات **-aat**. Many Arabic plurals are *irregular* and have to be learned individually.

TOPIC 4: Where is it?

My room

1. Tear out Game Card 4 at the back of your book and cut out the the small pictures of items around the house (leave the sentence-build cards at the bottom of the sheet for the moment).

2. Stick the pictures wherever you like on the scene below.

3. Cut out the sentence-build cards from Game Card 4. Make as many sentences as you can describing your room. For example:

| . | السرير | فوق | صورة | هناك |

hunaaka Soora fawq as-sareer.

Key Words

كبير **kabeer**	*big*	طويل **Taweel**	*tall/long*
صغير **Sagheer**	*small*	قصير **qaSeer**	*short*
قديم **qadeem**	*old*	غالٍ **ghaalee**	*expensive*
جديد **jadeed**	*new*	رخيص **rakheeS**	*inexpensive*
جدا **jiddan**	*very*		

Can you remember?

Cover the Key Words panel on this page. Then see if you can write out the pronunciation and meaning of the words below, as in the example.

رخيص **r a k h e e S** *inexpensive*   قصير **q _ _ _ _ r** _____

طويل **T _ _ _ _ l** _____   غالٍ **g _ _ _ _ _ e** _____

صغير **S _ _ _ _ _ r** _____   كبير **k _ _ _ _ r** _____

قديم **q _ _ _ _ m** _____   جديد **j _ _ _ _ d** _____

جدا **j _ _ _ _ n** _____

Language Focus

⊙ ⊙ ⊙ ⊙ ⊙ Descriptive words, or *adjectives*, come <u>after</u> the word they are describing. If the noun being described is feminine, the adjective will also have the feminine ة **-a** ending:

> بيت كبير **bayt kabeer** *(a) big house* (masc.)
>
> سيارة جديدة **sayyaara jadeeda** *(a) new car* (fem.)

⊙ ⊙ ⊙ ⊙ If you want to say <u>the</u> big house, etc., then both the noun and the adjective need to start with الـ **al-**:

> البيت الكبير **al-bayt al-kabeer** *the big house*
>
> السيارة الجديدة **as-sayyaara al-jadeeda** *the new car*

⊙ ⊙ ⊙ Note that when only the noun has الـ **al-** then the meaning changes. By putting a definite noun (with الـ **al-**) followed by an indefinite adjective (without الـ **al-**), a sentence is created meaning *The house is big*, etc:

> البيت كبير. **al-bayt kabeer.** *The house is big.*
>
> الكنبة جديدة. **al-kanaba jadeeda.** *The sofa is new.*
>
> الشاي رخيص. **ash-shaay rakheeS.** *The tea is inexpensive.*

⊙ ⊙ جدا **jiddan** (*very*) comes after the adjective:

> كرسي صغير جدا **kursee Sagheer jiddan** *(a) very small chair*
>
> الكتاب قديم جدا. **al-kitaab qadeem jiddan.** *The book is very old.*

⊙ Note the unusual ending of غال (*expensive*), formally pronounced **ghaalin**, but more commonly pronounced **ghaalee**. The feminine is غالية (**ghaalya**).

> قلم غالٍ **qalam ghaalee** *(an) expensive pen*
>
> سيارة غالية **sayyaara ghaalya** *(an) expensive car*

TOPIC 5: What's it like?

What does it mean?

Match the Arabic with the pictures. Then read the Arabic out loud and write the English next to each, as in the example.

قهوة صغيرة _____

صورة غالية _____

كلب صغير *(a) small dog* _____

كنبة جديدة _____

بيت صغير _____

سيارة قديمة جدا _____

سندويتش كبير _____

شجر طويل جدا _____

TOPIC 5: What's it like?

Listen and check

TRACK NUMBER
24

Listen to the conversation at the car rental company and decide if these sentences are true or false.

	True	False
1 The conversation takes place in the evening.	❏	❏
2 The woman wants to rent a car.	❏	❏
3 She thinks the Mercedes is very expensive.	❏	❏
4 She thinks the Fiat is too big.	❏	❏
5 She likes the Peugot.	❏	❏
6 Her name is Amira Zidan.	❏	❏
7 She's from Amman in Jordan.	❏	❏

Unscramble the sentences

Look at the scrambled sentences below and write the correct order.

Example:

a	b	d	c
صبـاح	الخير	سيارة	أريد

3
❏	❏	❏	❏
كبيرة	أريد	جدا	سيارة

1
❏	❏	❏
سامي	اسمي	أميرة

4
❏	❏	❏	❏
هذه	السيارة	غالية	جدا

2
❏	❏	❏
من	أنا	تونس

Language Focus

You already know the Arabic pronouns **ana/anta** (**anti**)/**huwa/hiya** (*I/you/he/she*) and the possessive endings **-ee/-ak(-ik)** (*my/your*). Now here are the other pronouns and possessive endings:

		pronoun		possessive ending
I	أنا **ana**	ي **-ee**:	اسمي **ismee** *my name*
you (masc.)	أنت **anta**	ك **-ak**:	قلمك **qalamak** *your (masc.) pen*
you (fem.)	أنت **anti**	ك **-ik**:	بلدك **baladik** *your (fem.) country*
he	هو **huwa**	ـه **-uh**:	كتابه **kitaabuh** *his book*
she	هي **hiya**	ـها **-haa**:	سريرها **sareerhaa** *her bed*
we	نحن **naHnu**	ـنا **-naa**:	بيتنا **baytnaa** *our house*
you (pl.)	أنتم **antum**	ـكم **-kum**:	غرفكم **ghurafkum** *your (pl.) rooms*
they	هم **hum**	ـهم **-hum**:	بيوتهم **buyoothum** *their houses*

Notice that there are three ways of saying *you* and *your* depending on whether you are talking to a male (أنت **anta**), a female (أنت **anti**) or a group (أنتم **antum**).

You can combine the possessive endings with the word عند **'inda** (*with/at*) to express the meaning of "having" something:

عندنا سيارة جديدة. **'indanaa sayyaara jadeeda.**
We have a new car.

سمير عنده بيت في لندن. **sameer 'induh bayt fee lundun.**
Sameer has a house in London.

The final **a** is removed from عند **'inda** when ي **-ee**, ك **-ak/-ik**, or ـه **-uh** are added:

عندي كلب كبير. **'indee kalb kabeer.** *I have a big dog.*

هل عندك قلم؟ **hal 'indak qalam?** *Do you have a pen?*

Now you can take part in a conversation with the car rental company. Follow the prompts on your audio CD.

25

TOPIC 5: What's it like?

Key Words

TRACK NUMBER

26

جميل jameel	beautiful	شعر sha'r	hair
قبيح qabeeH	ugly	رأس ra's	head
سمين sameen	fat	أنف anf	nose
رفيع rafee'	thin	فم fam	mouth
غريب ghareeb	strange	ذيل THayl	tail

By now you're probably feeling much more confident about reading and speaking Arabic. Maybe you'd like to try writing the script for yourself. If so, make sure you get hold of a guide to handwriting the Arabic script or ask a native speaker to show you. It's not always obvious how to form the letters or how to join them by looking at the printed script.

TOPIC 5: What's it like?

Which word?

Circle the correct word to match the translation,
as in the example.

1 فأر   باب   (رأس)   فم   *head*

2 رخيص   غريب   غالٍ   غرفة   *strange*

3 سرير   سيارة   صغير   سمين   *fat*

4 باب   فأر   فم   قلم   *mouth*

5 ذيل   صورة   باب   بيت   *tail*

6 صغير   شعر   شجرة   شباك   *hair*

7 جديد   جدا   جميل   قبيح   *beautiful*

8 أنف   فرن   فم   أقلام   *nose*

9 رخيص   رفيع   سرير   غريب   *thin*

10 قصير   قلم   قديم   قبيح   *ugly*

TOPIC 5: What's it like?

At the pet show

Can you use the words in the box to complete the description
of these pets?

3 هذا	2 جدا	1 أنفها
6 القطة	5 قصير	4 طويل

هذه ___6___ جميلة. ذيلها _____ جدا و _____ صغير وجميل.

_____ الكلب قبيح وغريب. ذيله _____ وانفه كبير _____!

What does it look like?

What does the alien look like? Make as many sentences as you can describing what this creature looks like.

We've included a checklist of features you could describe and adjectives you could use.

Example:

هو سمين وفمه صغير.

huwa sameen wa-famuh Sagheer.

He's fat and his mouth is small.

جميل *beautiful*

قبيح *ugly*

سمين *fat*

رفيع *thin*

كبير *big*

صغير *small*

طويل *tall/long*

قصير *short*

غريب *strange*

جدا *very*

شعر *hair*

رأس *head*

أنف *nose*

فم *mouth*

ذيل *tail*

What do you have?

1. Cut out the picture cards from Game Card 5 and put them in a bag.

2. Cut out set 2 adjective cards and put them in a different bag.

3. Pull out one card from each bag without looking.

4. Make a sentence to match the cards you have chosen, for example:

عندي كمبيوتر قديم.

'indee kumbiyootir qadeem.

(*I have an old computer.*)

Don't forget to make the adjective feminine if the noun is feminine:

عندي سيارة جديدة.

'indee sayyaara jadeeda.

(*I have a new car.*)

5. Keep playing until all the cards have been chosen.

6. You can put the cards back in the bag and start again – each time the sentences will be different.

GAME CARD 5 (see page 53)

Picture cards:

Adjective cards:

غريب	قبيح	طويل	جديد
سمين	قصير	صغير	قديم
رخيص	غال	كبير	جميل

قديم

Key Words

مطار **maTaar**   airport
(pl. **-aat**)

مدرسة **madrasa**   school
(pl. **madaaris**)

فندق **funduq**   hotel
(pl. **fanaadiq**)

بنك **bank**   bank
(pl. **bunook**)

مطعم **maT'am**   restaurant
(pl. **maTaa'im**)

محطّة **maHaTTa**   station
(pl. **-aat**)

حديقة **Hadeeqa**   park
(pl. **Hadaa'iq**)

جسر **jisr**   bridge
(pl. **jusoor**)

شارع **shaari'**   street
(pl. **shawaari'**)

شارع الملك   Malik (King) Street
shaari' al-malik

متحف **matHaf**   museum
(pl. **mataaHif**)

أين...؟ **ayna...?**   where's...?

TRACK NUMBER
28

You are new in town and are asking an Arabic-speaking friend about the facilities. Follow the prompts on your audio CD.

Language Focus

◉ ◉ ◉ ◉ ◉ Modern Arabic has many loan words imported from other languages, particularly English. You have already met some, such as كمبيوتر **kumbiyootir,** تليفون **tilifoon,** بنك **bank,** and سندويتش **sandawitsh.** Other examples of words you will recognize easily are راديو **raadyo** (*radio*), فيديو **feedyo** (*video*), كولا **kola** (*cola*), and تاكسي **taaksee** (*taxi*).

◉ ◉ ◉ ◉ In an attempt to minimize foreign influence on the language, "purer" Arabic alternatives have developed for most of these words, for example, مصرف **maSraf** for bank (literally "place for changing [money]"), آلة حاسبة **aala Haasiba** ("calculating instrument") for computer, and سيارة أجرة **sayyaarat ujra** ("car for rent") for taxi. These alternatives are sometimes used in more formal language.

Questions and answers

Match the questions with their answers, as in the example.

الفندق أمام الجسر.

هي قريبة من هنا.

الجسر بجانب المحطة.

البنك في شارع الملك.

نعم، مطعم كبير.

أين الجسر؟

أين فندق الأميرة؟

هل هناك مطعم في الفندق؟

أين المدرسة؟

أين البنك؟

Key Words

تاكسي **taksee** — *taxi*

(pl. **-yaat**)

طائرة **Taa'ira** — *airplane*

(pl. **-aat**)

أتوبيس **otobees** — *bus*

(pl. **-aat**)

مركب **markib** — *boat*

(pl. **maraakib**)

قطار **qiTaar** — *train*

(pl. **-aat**)

دراجة **darraaja** — *bicycle*

(pl. **-aat**)

TRACK NUMBER **29**

Language Focus

⊙ ⊙ ⊙ ⊙ ⊙ To express how you travel, use بـ **bi-** (*by/with*) + means of transportation. بـ **bi-** is written joined to the following word.

⊙ ⊙ ⊙ ⊙ When talking in general, Arabic tends to use the definite الـ **al-**. When combined with بـ **bi-** the combination becomes بالـ **bil-** with the "l" assimilating if the following word starts with a sun letter (see page 34):

بالقطار **bil-qiTaar** *by train*   بالأتوبيس **bil-otobees** *by bus*

التاكسي **bit-taksee** *by taxi*   بالدراجة **bid-darraaja** *by bicycle*

بالمركب **bil-markib** *by boat*   بالطائرة **biT-Taa'ira** *by airplane*

TOPIC 6: How do I get there?

Word Square

Can you find the 7 different means of transportation in the word square?
Write out the meaning for the words you have found.

س	ب	ـئـ	ة	ر	ا	ي	س
ر	ـا	ط	قـ	جـ	و	ـئـ	ل
س	ي	ب	و	تـ	أ	ز	ظـ
ي	جـ	ي	م	ب	ك	ر	مـ
ع	تـ	ج	ل	س	م	أ	تـ
ة	جـ	ا	ر	د	ب	شـ	ضـ
ة	ر	ـئـ	ا	ط	و	تـ	أ
ع	مـ	ي	س	ك	ا	تـ	شـ

car _____

_____

_____

_____

_____

_____

Language Focus

⊙ ⊙ ⊙ ⊙ ⊙ The **hamza** (ء), which appears on or under **alif** at the beginning of a word, can also be found in the middle of words, usually written on a **sinna** ("tooth"): ـئـ. You pronounce the **hamza** as a breath between the two syllables.

⊙ ⊙ ⊙ ⊙ Words you have met which include this spelling feature are:

طائرة	**Taa'ira** *airplane*		حدائق	**Hadaa'iq** *parks*	
مائدة	**maa'ida** *table*		حقائب	**Haqaa'ib** *bags*	
موائد	**mawaa'id** *tables*		الجزائر	**al-jazaa'ir** *Algeria*	

TOPIC 6: How do I get there?

Key Words

TRACK NUMBER 30

لو سمحت!   *excuse me!*

law samaHt (fem: **law samaHti**)

على اليمين   *on the right*

'ala l-yameen

... من أين؟   *How do I get to ...?*

... min ayna?

على اليسار   *on the left*

'ala l-yasaar

يمين   **yameen**   *right*

على طول   *(go) straight ahead*

'ala Tool

يسار   **yasaar**   *left*

أول شارع   *the first street*

awwal shaari'

هنا   **huna**   *here*

ثم   **thumma**   *then*

ثاني شارع   *the second street*

thaanee shaari'

بعد ذلك   *after that*

ba'da THaalik

TRACK NUMBER 31

○ *Ask for directions to places around town.*
○ *Follow the prompts on your audio CD.*

Language Focus

◎ ◎ ◎ ◎ ◎ As well as asking the question ؟من أين ... ... **min ayna?** (literally ... *from where?*), you'll need to understand basic directions. In addition to the phrases in the Key Words panel, you might also hear the instruction ... خذ **khuTH ...** (*take ...*) used to give directions:

خذ تاكسي من هنا. **khuTH taaksee min huna.**
Take a taxi from here.

خذ أول شارع على اليمين. **khuTH awwal shaari' 'ala l-yameen.**
Take the first street on the right.

◎ ◎ ◎ ◎ When talking to a female, add **-ee** to the end of the instruction – خذي **khuTHee:**

خذي ثاني شارع على اليسار. **khuTHee thaanee shaari' 'ala l-yasaar.** *Take the second street on the left.*

◎ ◎ ◎ *At*, as in *at the bridge*, is عند **'inda** which you already know from expressing possession:

خذ الأتوبيس عند الجسر. **khuTH al-otoobees 'inda l-bank.**
Take the bus at the bridge.

خذي أول شارع على اليسار عند المتحف.
khuTHee awwal shaari' 'ala l-yasaar 'inda l-matHaf.
Take (fem.) the first street on the left at the museum.

ACTIVITIES

Which way?

Make questions and answers, as in the example.

لو سمحت، المحطة من أين؟

law samaHt, al-maHaTTa min ayna?

Excuse me, how do I get to the station?

خذ أول شارع على اليسار.

khuTH awwal shaari' 'ala l-yasaar

Take the first street on the left.

Around town

Below is a plan of a small town with some landmarks shown.
Starting from *You are here*, try to give directions to the following places:

المحطة	فندق كريم	الحديقة	محطة الأتوبيس
the station	Karim Hotel	the park	the bus station

For example, your directions to the station could be something like this:

على طول من هنا وبعد ذلك خذ أول شارع على اليمين عند البنك.

المحطة قريبة من الجسر. **'ala Tool min huna wa-ba'da** THaalik khuTH **awwal shaari' 'ala l-yameen 'inda l-bank. al-maHaTTa qareeba min al-jisr.**

Go straight ahead from here and after that take the first street on the right at the bank. The station is near the bridge.

ACTIVITIES

Unscramble the conversation

Can you put this conversation in the correct order?

ORDER: e,_____

Did you also work out whether the person asking is male or female?
Check your answer with the conversation on your audio CD.

TRACK NUMBER
32

TOPIC 6: How do I get there?

Town Planning

TRACK NUMBER
33

1. Cut out the pictures of places around town from Game Card 6.

2. Listen to the first set of directions for the bank on your audio CD.

3. Pause the CD and stick the picture of the bank in the correct place on the town map on your game card.

4. Listen to the next set of directions and stick down the appropriate picture.

5. Repeat for all the directions until you have all your pictures stuck down on the map.

6. Looking at the completed map, you could try to give directions to the various places yourself. For example:

خذ ثاني شارع على اليسار.

البنك على اليمين بجانب المدرسة.

khuth thaanee shaari' 'ala l-yasaar.

al-bank 'ala l-yameen bi-jaanib al-madrasa.

(*Take the second street on the left.*
The bank is on the right next to the school.)

Key Words

TRACK NUMBER
34

زوجة **zawja**	*wife*	
زوج **zawj**	*husband*	
أم **umm**	*mother*	
أب **ab**	*father*	
أخت **ukht** (pl. **akhawaat**)	*sister*	

أخ **akh** (pl. **ikhwa**)	*brother*	
طفل **Tifl** (pl. **aTfaal**)	*child*	
ابنة **ibna** (pl. **banaat**)	*daughter*	
ابن **ibn** (pl. **abnaa'**)	*son*	

Find a photograph album and point to your relatives and friends, saying who they are in Arabic. For example: هذا أخي. haaTHa akhee. (This is my brother.); هذه سارة وزوجها سامي. haaTHihi saara wa-zawjhaa saamee. (This is Sarah and her husband Sammy.) Look back at page 48 if you want to review the possessive endings.

TOPIC 7: Who's this?

Language Focus

◉ ◉ ◉ ◉ ◉ You can use عند 'inda to talk about your family:

> عندي أخ اسمه مارك. 'indee akh ismuh maark.
> *I have a brother whose name is Mark. (lit: "... his name is Mark")*
>
> هل عندك أطفال؟ hal 'indak aTfaal?
> *Do you have children?*

◉ ◉ ◉ ◉ ◉ The opposite is ليس عند laysa 'inda:

> سميرة ليس عندها أخ. sameera laysa 'indahaa akh.
> *Sameera doesn't have a brother.*
>
> ليس عندنا بنات. laysa 'indanaa banaat.
> *We don't have any daughters.*

What does it mean?

Join the Arabic to the pronunciation and the English, as in the example.

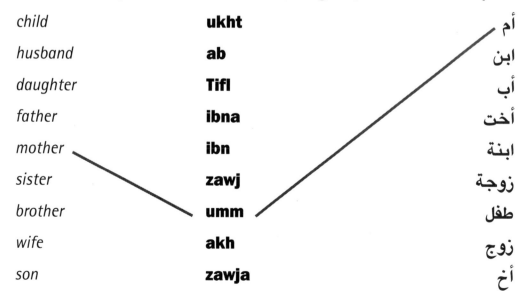

child	ukht	أم
husband	ab	ابن
daughter	Tifl	أب
father	ibna	أخت
mother	ibn	ابنة
sister	zawj	زوجة
brother	umm	طفل
wife	akh	زوج
son	zawja	أخ

IDAAFA

Language Focus

⊚ ⊚ ⊚ ⊚ ⊚ You know how to use possessive endings: بنتي **bintee** *my daughter*; زوجك **zawjik** *your husband*, etc.

⊚ ⊚ ⊚ ⊚ ⊚ To express possession using a noun (the equivalent of the English *'s* or *of* as in *Ahmed's son* or *the door of the school*), Arabic puts the two words directly together in the order *possessed + possessor*. This possessive construction is called إضافة **iDaafa** (*addition*). The <u>first</u> noun in an **iDaafa** doesn't have the article الـ **al**, even if the meaning is definite:

> ابن أحمد **ibn aHmad**
> *son + Ahmed = Ahmed's son*
>
> باب المدرسة **baab al-madrasa**
> *door + the school = [the] door of the school*
>
> أنف الكلب **anf al-kalb**
> *nose + the dog = the dog's nose*

⊚ ⊚ When feminine nouns ending in **taa marbooTa** (ة) are the <u>first</u> noun in an **iDaafa** or have a possessive ending, the **taa marbooTa** (ة) is pronounced **-at** rather than **-a**. The **taa marbooTa** is spelled as a regular **taa** (ـت) when an ending is added:

زوجة **zawja**	زوجتي **zawjatee**	زوجة أحمد **zawjat aHmad**
(a) wife	*my wife*	*Ahmed's wife*
مدينة **madeena**	مدينتهم **madeenathum**	مدينة دمشق **madeenat dimashq**
(a) city	*their city*	*(the) city of Damascus*

⊚ ⊚ Take note of أب **ab** (*father*) and أخ **akh** (*brother*) which add an ـو **-oo** when they are the **first** word in an **iDaafa** or have a possessive ending (except **-ee**):

> أبو سارة **aboo saara** *Sarah's father*   أبونا **aboona** *our father*
> أخو علي **akhoo 'ali** *Ali's brother*   أخوها **akhoohaa** *her brother*

TOPIC 7: Who's this?

Family Tree

Make up eight sentences about this family, as in the example.

زينة هي زوجة أحمد.

zayna hiya zajwat aHmad.

Zayna is Ahmed's wife.

Anwar's family

Listen to Anwar answering questions about
his family. Circle the correct names on the family tree, as in the example.

Questions and answers

Now read the questions on the right and then match them to the answers on the left
that Anwar gave, as in the example.

اسمه صفوان.	ما اسمك؟
اسمها صباح سالم.	ما اسم أمك؟
أنا من بيروت.	وأبوك، ما اسمه؟
نعم، عندي أخ.	أنت من أين؟
اسمي أنور دياب.	هل عندك أخوات؟
اسمه محمد دياب.	هل عندك أخوة؟
لا، ليس عندي أخوات.	وأخوك، ما اسمه؟

TOPIC 7: Who's this?

Language Focus

If you want to introduce someone, you can use هذا... **haатна...** for males or ...هذه **haатнihi...** to introduce females:

هذه ابنتي شادية. **haатнihi ibnatee shaadya.**
This is my daughter, Shadya.

هذا أخي صفوان. **haатна akhee Safwaan.**
This is my brother, Safwaan.

Who's this? is من هذا؟ / من هذه؟ **man haатна?/man haатнihi?**
And remember how to say *pleased to meet you* from topic 1?:

فرصة سعيدة. **furSa sa'eeda.**
Pleased to meet you. (literally: "happy occasion")

So now we can put all that together in a short conversation:

أهلا يا سمير. **ahlan yaa sameer.** *Hello Sameer.*

أهلا يا جاين. من هذا؟ **ahlan yaa jaayin. man haатна?**
Hello Jane. Who's this?

هذا أخي مارك. **haатна akhee maark.** *This is my brother, Mark.*

أهلا يا مارك. فرصة سعيدة. **ahlan yaa maark. furSa saa'ida.**
Hello Mark. Pleased to meet you.

فرصة سعيدة يا سمير. **furSa saa'ida yaa sameer.**
Pleased to meet you, Sameer.

TRACK NUMBER **36**

Now introduce <u>your</u> family. Follow the prompts on your audio CD.

TOPIC 7: Who's this?

Key Words

واحد **waaHid**	*one*		ستة **sitta**	*six*
اثنان **ithnaan**	*two*		سبعة **sab'a**	*seven*
ثلاثة **thalaatha**	*three*		ثمانية **thamaanya**	*eight*
أربعة **arba'a**	*four*		تسعة **tis'a**	*nine*
خمسة **khamsa**	*five*		عشرة **'ashara**	*ten*

Language Focus

⊙ ⊙ ⊙ ⊙ ⊙ Although western figures are sometimes used in the Middle East, you will also see these Arabic numerals:

0	1	2	3	4	5	6	7	8	9	10
٠	١	٢	٣	٤	٥	٦	٧	٨	٩	١٠

⊙ ⊙ ⊙ ⊙ A peculiarity of Arabic numbers is that the figures are written left to right, i.e. in the opposite direction to the rest of the script:

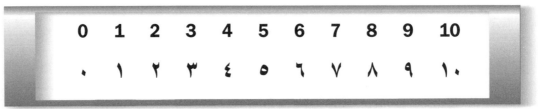

10 = ١٠   65 = ٦٥   3947 = ٣٩٤٧

How many?

Match the numbers with the figures, as in the example.

تسعة	٣
اثنان	١٠
سبعة	٨
واحد	٥
أربعة	١
ستة	٩
ثمانية	٢
ثلاثة	٦
عشرة	٧
خمسة	٤

Arabic sums

Circle the correct answer to these sums, as in the example.

1 واحد + ثلاثة = ‏ واحد اثنان ثلاثة (أربعة) خمسة ستة سبعة ثمانية تسعة عشرة

2 أربعة + اثنان = ‏ واحد اثنان ثلاثة أربعة خمسة ستة سبعة ثمانية تسعة عشرة

3 اثنان × أربعة = ‏ واحد اثنان ثلاثة أربعة خمسة ستة سبعة ثمانية تسعة عشرة

4 خمسة + ثلاثة = ‏ واحد اثنان ثلاثة أربعة خمسة ستة سبعة ثمانية تسعة عشرة

5 ستة – ثلاثة = ‏ واحد اثنان ثلاثة أربعة خمسة ستة سبعة ثمانية تسعة عشرة

6 سبعة + ثلاثة = ‏ واحد اثنان ثلاثة أربعة خمسة ستة سبعة ثمانية تسعة عشرة

7 تسعة – أربعة = ‏ واحد اثنان ثلاثة أربعة خمسة ستة سبعة ثمانية تسعة عشرة

8 ثمانية + اثنان = ‏ واحد اثنان ثلاثة أربعة خمسة ستة سبعة ثمانية تسعة عشرة

9 ثلاثة × ثلاثة = ‏ واحد اثنان ثلاثة أربعة خمسة ستة سبعة ثمانية تسعة عشرة

10 ستة – خمسة = ‏ واحد اثنان ثلاثة أربعة خمسة ستة سبعة ثمانية تسعة عشرة

Language Focus

⊙ ⊙ ⊙ ⊙ ⊙ Arabic has a special *dual* form used only for talking about two things. Instead of using اثنان **ithnaan** (*two*) followed by a plural noun, a dual ending ان **aan** is added to the end of the singular noun:

طفل	طفلان	ثلاثة أطفال
Tifl	**Tiflaan**	**thalaathat aTfaal**
(a) child	*two children*	*three children*

My family

Make sentences about your own family, using عندي and ليس عندي, for example:

عندي أختان. **'indee ukhtaan.** *I have two sisters.*

ليس عندي أطفال. **laysa 'indee aTfaal.** *I don't have any children.*

Look back at page 64 to remind yourself of the members of the family.

Listen and speak

TRACK NUMBER 38

Now imagine you are with some of your family looking for the station and you meet an Arab friend.

Prepare carefully the information below you will need to take part in the conversation. Then go to your audio CD and see how you get on introducing your family.

　1 Think of two members of your family – one male and one female. For example, your husband and your daughter; or your brother and your mother.

　2 How would you introduce them and tell someone their names in Arabic?

　3 How do you ask *How do I get to the station?*

　4 How do you say *thank you* and *goodbye*

You can repeat the conversation, but this time use two different members of your family and ask how to get to the bus stop.

TOPIC 7: Who's this?

Bingo!

1. Cut out the small number tokens and the bingo cards on Game Card 7.

2. Find 16 buttons for each player or make 16 small blank pieces of card (to cover the squares on the bingo card).

3. Put the tokens into a bag and shake thoroughly.

4. Pull out a number token and say the number out loud in Arabic.

5. If you have that number on your card, cover the square with a button or blank piece of card. If you have more than one square with that number, you can only cover one.

6. Put the number token back in the bag and shake again.

7. Repeat steps 3–6 until you have all the squares covered on the bingo card. Then you can shout: كسبت! **kasabt!** (*I've won!*)

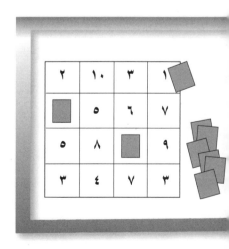

Key Words

TRACK NUMBER

39

مدرس **mudarris**   *teacher*

(pl. **-oon**)

صياد **SayyaaD**   *fisherman*

(pl. **-oon**)

طالب **Taalib**   *student*

(pl. **Tullaab**)

مهندس **muhandis**   *engineer*

(pl. **-oon**)

طبيب **Tabeeb**   *doctor*

(pl. **aTibbaa'**)

محاسب **muHaasib**   *accountant*

(pl. **-oon**)

طباخ **Tabbaakh**   *cook/chef*

(pl. **-oon**)

سائق **saa'iq**   *driver*

(pl. **-oon**)

موظف **muwaZZaf**   *employee*

(pl. **-oon**)

ممثل **mumaththil**   *actor*

(pl. **-oon**)

If your occupation or those of your family aren't listed here, try to find out what they are in Arabic.

What does it mean?

Join the Arabic to the pronunciation and the English, as in the example.

English	Pronunciation	Arabic
employee	**Sayyaad**	طبيب
accountant	**muhandis**	طالب
actor	**Tabeeb**	محاسب
driver	**mudarris**	موظف
fisherman	**muHaasib**	مدرس
engineer	**Taalib**	مهندس
doctor	**saa'iq**	صياد
cook/chef	**mumaththil**	سائق
teacher	**Tabbaakh**	ممثل
student	**muwaZZaf**	طباخ

The tools of the trade

Match the jobs to the tools of the trade, as in the example.

Language Focus

If you want to refer to a female profession, you need to add ة -a:

مدرس **mudarris** *male teacher* → مدرسة **mudarrisa** *female teacher*

طبيب **Tabeeb** *male doctor* → طبيبة **Tabeeba** *female doctor*

Many professions can be made plural by adding the ending ون -oon. The -oon ending is one of only two regular plurals, the other being -aat (see page 40). -oon is used <u>only</u> to refer to groups of people and is common when describing professions and nationalities.

موظف **muwaZZaf** *employee* → موظفون
muwaZZafoon *employees*

طباخ **Tabbaakh** *cook* → طباخون
Tabbaakhoon *cooks*

أمريكي **amreekee** *American* → أمريكيون
amreekeeoon *Americans*

The -aat plural ending is used to describe a group of only females: موظفات **muwaZZifaat** *(female employees)*, طباخات **Tabbaakhaat** *(female cooks)*.

To ask someone about their job you can use the question ما عملك؟ **maa 'amalak?**, or **maa 'amalik?** for a female (literally *what your work?*).

ما عملك؟ أنا مدرس.
maa 'amalak? ana mudarris.
What do you (masculine) do? I'm a teacher.

ما عملك؟ أنا محاسبة.
maa 'amalik? ana muHaasiba.
What do you (feminine) do? I'm an accountant.

Listen and note

TRACK NUMBER
40

Listen to two people telling you about themselves
and fill in the details in English on the forms below.

First name: ....*Dina*............................

Family name:...

Nationality: ....

Name of spouse: ....

No. of children: ....

Occupation: ....

First name: ....

Family name:..

Nationality: ....

Name of spouse: ....

No. of children: ....

Occupation: ....

Your turn to speak

TRACK NUMBER
41

Now you give same information about yourself.
Follow the prompts on your audio CD.

What's the answer?

Match the questions to the answers.

For example: a6

Which word?

Write the correct number of the word in the box to complete the description, as in the example.

اسمي هاري وأنا ــــــــ 2 ــــــــ. أنا من

ملبورن في ــــــــ. زوجتي

ــــــــ جوسلين و ــــــــ ابن

اسمه ــــــــ.

1 سامي	2 ممثل	
3 اسمها	4 أستراليا	5 عندنا

Key Words

maSna‘ مصنع (pl. **maSaani‘**)	factory	**maktab** مكتب (pl. **makaatib**)	office
mustashfa مستشفى (pl. **-yaat**)	hospital	**jaami‘a** جامعة (pl. **jaami‘aat**)	college/ university
maHall محل (pl. **-aat**)	store	**sharika** شركة (pl. **-aat**)	company/ business
masraH مسرح (pl. **masaariH**)	theater	*Look back as well at the Key Words on page 54 for other places of work.*	

Language Focus

To describe where you work or who you work for, you can say أنا أعمل في... **ana a'mal fee...** (*I work in...*):

أنا طبيب وأنا أعمل في مستشفى صغير قريب من بيتي.
ana Tabeeb wa-ana a'mal fee mustashfa Sagheer qareeb min baytee. *I'm a doctor and I work in a small hospital near my house.*

أنا محاسبة وأنا أعمل في شركة كبيرة في القاهرة.
ana muHaasiba wa-ana a'mal fee sharika kabeera fil-qaahira. *I'm an accountant and I work in a large company in Cairo.*

Word Square

Can you find the 8 different work places in the word square?
Write out the meaning for the words you have found.

ط	بـ	م	عـ	ط	مـ	ي	ق
ر	ى	فـ	شـ	تـ	سـ	مـ	لـ
س	بـ	تـ	كـ	مـ	أ	ز	ظ
ي	جـ	يـ	مَ	عـ	نـ	صـ	مـ
ة	سـ	ر	د	مـ	م	أ	تـ
ة	لـ	حـ	بـ	كـ	ر	مـ	ضـ
ك	نـ	بـ	ﺎ	ط	و	تـ	أ
ع	مـ	ي	سـ	ح	ر	سـ	مـ

factory _____

_____

_____

_____

_____

_____

_____

_____

Now make sentences for each of the work-places, as in the example:

أنا مهندس وأنا أعمل في مصنع.

ana muhandis wa-ana a'mal fee maSna'.

I'm an engineer and I work in a factory.

TOPIC 8: What do you do?

What are they saying?

Match the people with what they are saying. For example: **1d**

2 ‎أنا أعمل في مطعم في القاهرة.

1 ‎أنا أعمل في مدرسة في إنجلترا.

4 ‎أنا أعمل في محل في باريس.

3 ‎أنا أعمل في بنك أمريكي.

6 ‎أنا أعمل في مصنع في دمشق.

5 ‎أنا أعمل في مسرح في كندا.

a

b

c

d

e

f

Listen and speak

TRACK NUMBER 43

Imagine you are a chef. You're meeting someone for the first time and they are asking you about yourself.

Prepare carefully the information below you will need to take part in the conversation. Then go to your audio CD and see how you get on talking about yourself.

1 Your name is Ali Al-Halabee (علي الحلبي).

2 You're from Damascus.

3 You're a chef.

4 You work in a Lebanese restaurant in New York.

5 You have three daughters.

6 Your wife is a teacher in a big school.

Which word?

Now write the correct number of the word in the box to complete the description, as in the example.

4 بنات	3 في	2 سوريا	1 كبيرة
8 طباخ	7 الحلبي	6 عندنا	5 مطعم

أنا علي ____7____ من دمشق في ____ ____ . أنا أعمل ____

مدينة نيويورك. أنا ____ في ____ ____ لبناني هناك. زوجتي مدرسة في

مدرسة ____ قريبة من المطعم. ____ ثلاث ____ : سارة، منى وفاطمة.

Where do I work?

1. ↓ Tear out the work-place picture cards and profession word cards on Game Card 8.

2. ↓ Turn the cards face down on a table, with the pictures on one end of the table and the words on the other.

3. ↓ Turn a word card and say ... أنا **ana ...** (*I'm a ...*) as appropriate, not fogetting to add the feminine ending if you are female, e.g. أنا مدرس/أنا مدرسة **ana mudarris/ ana mudarrisa** (*I'm a teacher*).

4. Then turn a picture card. If the work-place picture matches the profession, say ... أنا أعمل في **ana a'mal fi ...** (*I work in a/ an ...*), e.g. أنا أعمل في مدرسة **ana a'mal fee madrasa** (*I work in a school*).

5. If you turn a matching picture and say both sentences correctly you get to keep the cards. If you don't, you must turn the cards face down and try again.

6. The winner is the one who collects the most cards.

7. You can compete with a friend or challenge yourself against the clock.

(Review the vocabulary on pages 54, 56 and 74 before you play the game.)

TEST YOURSELF

○ ○ ○ ○ ○ This **Test Yourself** section reviews all the Arabic you have learned in this program. Have a go at the activities. If you find you have forgotten something, go back to the relevant topic(s) and look again at the **Key Words** and **Language Focus** panels.

May I have...?

Ask for the following, as in the example:

ممكن شاي من فضلك؟/أريد شاي من فضلك.
mumkin shaay min faDlak?/ureed shaay min faDlak.

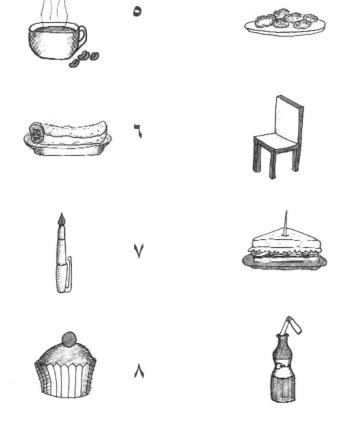

٥   ١

٦   ٢

٧   ٣

٨   ٤

Listen and check

Listen to Nour talking about herself and decide if
the following sentences are true or false.

TRACK NUMBER
44

		True	False
1	Nour is Syrian.	☐	☐
2	She comes from a small town.	☐	☐
3	She's a teacher.	☐	☐
4	She works in Kuwait.	☐	☐
5	Her husband is an engineer.	☐	☐
6	She has five children.	☐	☐

Which word?

Now write the correct number of the word in the box to
complete the description of Nour, as in the example.

اسمي ___8___ . _____ _____ من حلب، مدينة _____ _____ في سوريا.

أنا مدرسة _____ السعودية و _____ طبيب هناك في _____

قريب _____ المدرسة. عندنا أربعة _____ : ابن وثلاث بنات.

Can you try and make up a similar description about yourself?

Read and check

Look at the picture and decide if the sentences are true or false.
Look back at topics 4–6 if you are unsure of any of the words.

False   True

☐   ☐   ١ هناك بنك في الصورة.

☐   ☐   ٢ هناك مستشفى بجانب البنك.

☐   ☐   ٣ هناك مدرسة بجانب البنك.

☐   ☐   ٤ هناك كلب في الشارع.

☐   ☐   ٥ ليس هناك سيارات في الصورة.

☐   ☐   ٦ ليس هناك طائرات في الصورة.

☐   ☐   ٧ هناك قطة صغيرة فوق السيارة.

☐   ☐   ٨ هناك شجر طويل وراء المدرسة.

☐   ☐   ٩ هناك دراجة قديمة أمام المستشفى.

What does it mean?

Can you remember these words? Join the words and write the pronunciation next to the Arabic, as in the example

English	Arabic	Pronunciation
children	أبناء	_abnaa'_
husband	بنات	_____
sons	ابن	_____
daughter	أخ	_____
father	أم	_____
mother	أب	_____
sister	أخت	_____
brother	زوجة	_____
daughters	أطفال	_____
child	زوج	_____
wife	إخوة	_____
brothers	أخوات	_____
son	ابنة	_____
sisters	طفل	_____

How do you say it?

Now see if you can say these in Arabic, as in the example.

1 My husband is a doctor.

   zawjee Tabeeb. زوجي طبيب.

2 I have four children.

3 His son is an engineer.

4 Sameer's mother is from Saudi.

5 My wife's name is Jocelyn.

6 Her brother is an actor.

7 I don't have any sisters.

8 I have three daughters.

TEST YOURSELF

At the tourist office

TRACK NUMBER
45

Finally, you are going to test your new Arabic conversational skills by joining in the dialog on your audio CD.

You're going to ask for some information at a tourist information office.

To prepare, first see if you can remember these words and phrases. Write the English next to the Arabic, as in the example.

Arabic	English
مع السلامة	_goodbye_
شكرا	_____
وراء	_____
على اليمين	_____
على اليسار	_____
شارع	_____
أتوبيس	_____
قريب	_____
كبير	_____
متحف	_____
أين	_____
صباح الخير	_____

Now follow the prompts on your audio CD. Don't worry if you don't manage everything the first time around. Just keep repeating it until you are fluent.

⊙ ⊙ ⊙ ⊙ ⊙ Congratulations on successfully completing this introductory *Read and Speak* Arabic program. You have overcome the obstacle of learning an unfamiliar language and a different script. You should now have the confidence to enjoy using the Arabic you have learned. You have also acquired a sound basis from which to expand your language skills in whichever direction you choose. Good luck!

This **Reference** section gives an overview of the Arabic script and pronunciation. You can use it to refer to as you work your way through the *Read and Speak Arabic* program. Don't expect to take it all in from the beginning. *Read and Speak Arabic* is designed to build your confidence step by step as you progress through the topics. The details will start to fall into place gradually as you become more familiar with the Arabic script and language.

The Arabic script

The Arabic script is written from *right to left*, i.e. the opposite direction to English. The alphabet has 28 letters, no capitals, and – unlike English – words are generally spelled as they sound.

The letters in an Arabic word are "joined up" — you cannot "print" a word as you can in English. When the letters join to other letters they change their shape. The most common change is that letters lose their "tails" when joined to a following letter (on the right):

read this way ⟵

م + س = مس

ق + ل = قل

س + م = سم

ب + ر = بر

Because letters change their shape like this, they have an *initial*, a *medial* (middle) and a *final* form. For example, the letter ج (**jeem**) changes like this:

initial (at the beginning):   جر

medial (in the middle):   فجل

final (at the end):   هج

A few letters, such as ه (**haa**) and ك (**kaaf**), change their shapes more radically. In addition, six letters – و (**waw**), ا (**alif**), د (**daal**), ذ (**THaal**), ر (**raa**), and ز (**zay**) – only join to the letter before and *never* to the letter following and so hardly change shape at all.

You will find details of how the individual letters change their shape in the alphabet table on page 90.

The Arabic alphabet

⊚ ⊚ ⊚ ⊚ ⊚ The table below shows all the Arabic letters in the three positions, with the Arabic letter name, followed by the sound. Remember that this is just for reference and you shouldn't expect to take it all in at once. If you know the basic principles of how the Arabic script works, you will slowly come to recognize the individual letters.

	initial	medial	final		initial	medial	final		initial	medial	final
alif[1] a/u/i/aa	ا	ا	ا	zaa z	ز	ز	ز	qaaf q	قـ	ـقـ	ق
baa b	بـ	ـبـ	ـب	seen s	سـ	ـسـ	س	kaaf k	كـ	ـكـ	ك
taa t	تـ	ـتـ	ـت	sheen sh	شـ	ـشـ	ش	laam[2] l	لـ	ـلـ	ل
thaa th	ثـ	ـثـ	ـث	Saad S	صـ	ـصـ	ص	meem m	مـ	ـمـ	م
jaa j	جـ	ـجـ	ـج	Daad D	ضـ	ـضـ	ض	noon n	نـ	ـنـ	ن
Haa H	حـ	ـحـ	ـح	Taa T	طـ	ـطـ	ط	haa h	هـ	ـهـ	ه/ة
khaa kh	خـ	ـخـ	ـخ	Zaa Z	ظـ	ـظـ	ظ	waaw w/oo	و	ـو	و
daal d	د	د	د	'ayn '	عـ	ـعـ	ـع/ع	yaa y/ee	يـ	ـيـ	ي
THaal TH	ذ	ذ	ذ	ghayn gh	غـ	ـغـ	ـغ/غ				
raa r	ر	ر	ر	faa f	فـ	ـفـ	ـف				

(1) When **alif** begins a word it is usually written with a **hamza** sign <u>above</u> (أ) if the word starts with **a** or **u**; or <u>below</u> (إ) if the word starts with **i**. A **madda** sign is written above (آ) if the word starts with a long **aa**.

(2) Note the special combination when **alif** is written after **laam**: لا.

⊚ ⊚ ⊚ ⊚ In written Arabic, the three short vowels (**a, i, u**) and a sign showing a letter is doubled are not normally included as part of the main script. They can be written as symbols above or below the letter. The short **a** as a dash above the letter, the short **i** as a dash below, the short **u** as a comma-shape above. The doubled letter symbol (**shadda**) can be written as a small "w" shape above the letter. Here are some example of Arabic words including these symbols:

كِتَاب **kitaab** *book*   مَجلّة **majalla** *magazine*

شُبّاك **shubbaak** *window*   كَلب **kalb** *dog*

However, most written material omits these symbols making it important for you to be able to recognize a word without them. In this book we have not included the vowel and doubling symbols, but the pronunciation guide will show you how to say the word. You will find it more useful to be able to read the Arabic script without the symbols from the beginning as then you can recognize simple notices, advertisements and signs more easily.

Pronunciation

The pronunciation of Arabic varies depending on the region and the level of formality. We have steered a middle course, using a friendly standard pronunciation. We have avoided both colloquialisms and the finer grammatical embellishments of "high Arabic."

Many Arabic letters are pronounced in a similar way to their English equivalents. Some are less familiar. Pay special attention to these letters:

ص **(Saad);** ض **(Daad);** ط **(Taa);** ظ **(Zaa)**	emphatic letters, pronounced with the tongue on the roof of the mouth rather than up against the teeth – written with a capital letter in the pronunciation to distinguish them from their non-emphatic equivalents
ح **(Haa)**	pronounced as a breathy "*h*" – written with a capital in the pronunciation to distinguish it from the regular "*h*".
خ **(khaa)**	pronounced like the "*ch*" in the Yiddish *"chutzpah"*
ع **('ayn)**	the sound most often associated with Arabic, and the most difficult to produce: a sort of guttural "*ah*"-sound
غ **(ghayn)**	pronounced like the French throaty "*r*"
ث **(thaa);** ذ **(THaal)**	ث **(thaa)** is a soft "*th*" as in "*thin*" and ذ **(THaal)** is a hard "*th*" as in "*that*"
ء **(hamza)**	a strange "half letter." Not really pronounced at all, but has the effect of cutting short the previous letter
ة **(taa marbooTa)**	a version of (**taa**) that only appears at the end of words and is pronounced **a** or **at**.

You will find an introduction to the sounds of Arabic on track 1 of your audio.

Topic 1

Page 6
Check your answers with the Key Words panel on page 5.

Page 8: What are they saying?

Page 8: What do you hear?
You should have ticked boxes 2 and 5.

Page 10: What does it mean?
1d, 2f, 3e, 4a, 5b, 6c

Page 10: Which word?

الخير. ــــ2ــــ

أهلا. مساء ــــ5ــــ .

أنا ــــ1ــــ يوسف. ــــ3ــــ اسمك؟

اسمي ــــ4ــــ .

Page 11: What are their names?

Jane	جاين	Suzanne	سوزان
Nancy	نانسي	Tony	توني
Mark	مارك	Lucy	لوسي
Mary	ماري	Sam	سام

Page 12: In or out?
IN: Mark, Zayna, Sameer, Sam, Charles, Yoosef
OUT: Harry, Lucy, Fatima, Jane

Topic 2

Page 15: Where are the countries?

مصر 8   إيرلندا 3   أمريكا 2

كندا 1   بريطانيا 4   سوريا 6   العراق 7   أستراليا 5

Page 16: How do you say it?
Check your answers with the Key Words panel on page 14.

Page 16: Where are the cities?

دمشق في سوريا.   dimashq fee sooriya.

دبلن في إيرلندا.   dublin fee eerlanda.

لندن في بريطانيا.   lundun fee biriTaanya.

تورنتو في كندا.   torunto fee kanada.

القاهرة في مصر.   al-qaahira fee miSr.

واشنطن في أمريكا.   waashinTun fee amreeka.

نيو يورك في أمريكا.   nyoo yoork fee amreeka.

سيدني في أستراليا.   sidnee fee usturalya.

Page 17: Audio track 8
Yoosef: Cairo in Egypt; Lucy: Oxford near London; Sameer: Baghdad in Iraq; Harry: Toronto in Canada; Fatima: Damascus in Syria; Suzanne: Princeton near New York.

Page 18: Where are they from?

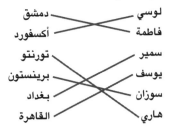

Page 20: Who's from where?

هو من أين؟ هو من نيو يورك في أمريكا. 1
huwa min ayna? huwa min nyoo yoork fee amreeka.

هي من أين؟ هي من القاهرة في مصر. 2
hiya min ayna? hiya min al-qaahira fee miSr.

هو من أين؟ هو من سيدني في أستراليا. 3
huwa min ayna? huwa min sidnee fee usturalya.

هي من أين؟ هي من تورنتو في كندا. 4
hiya min ayna? hiya min torunto fee kanada.

هو من أين؟ هو من بغداد في العراق. 5
huwa min ayna? huwa min baghdaad fil-'iraaq.

هو من أين؟ هو من دبلن في إيرلندا. 6
huwa min ayna? huwa min dublin fee eerlanda.

هي من أين؟ هي من لندن في بريطانيا. 7
hiya min ayna? hiya min lundun fee biriTaanya.

هو من أين؟ هو من دمشق في سوريا. 8
huwa min ayna? huwa min dimashq fee sooriya.

Page 21: Listen and Check
1 False; 2 False; 3 True; 4 True; 5 True; 6 False

Page 21: What does it mean?

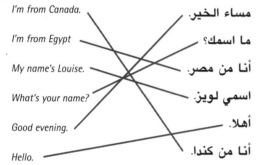

I'm from Canada.   مساء الخير.
I'm from Egypt   ما اسمك؟
My name's Louise.   أنا من مصر.
What's your name?   اسمي لويز.
Good evening.   أهلا.
Hello.   أنا من كندا.

Page 22: What does it mean?

My name's Zayna. اسمي زينة.   My name's Louise. اسمي لويز.
Where's he from? هو من أين؟   I'm from Canada. أنا من كندا.
He's from London. هو من لندن.   Munir is from Egypt. منير من مصر.
She's from America. هي من أمريكا.   What's your name? ما اسمك؟

Topic 3
Page 25
Check your answers with the Key Words panel on page 24.

Page 26: Word Square
bag, book, pen, chair, door, sofa, telephone, window

ج	ب	شِ	ـة	ب	ق	ح
ب	ل	كَ	و	غ	ل	ف
م	ب	ك	ع	ز	ظ	
ي	ج	ي	ق	ل	ذ	
ث	ح	م	س	ا	د	
ث	ز	ب	ك	شِ	ضِ	
ن	ف	ي	ل	ق	م	و
ي	س	ك	ن	ا	ل	

Page 26: Odd One Out

سمير * سوزان * (تليفزيون) * فاطمة
مائدة * كرسي * باب * (اسم)
مجلة * كتاب * قلم * (مساء)
مصر * (تليفون) * أمريكا * العراق
صباح الخير * (كنبة) * أهلا * مع السلامة

Page 28: What's this?
1e, 2b, 3f, 4c, 5h, 6d, 7a, 8g

Page 30: Who orders what?
Customer 1: coffee & falafel; Customer 2: tea & sandwich;
Customer 3: tea & pancake; Customer 4: sandwich & cake;
Customer 5: tea & falafel

Page 31: Unscramble the conversation
g, b, e, c, f, h, d, a

Topic 4
Page 35: What does it mean?
Check your answers with the Key Words panel on page 34.

Page 35: What can you see?

☐ كلب	☑ قطة
☐ ستار	☑ شباك
☐ شجر	☐ فرن
☐ سرير	☐ باب
☐ صورة	☑ حقيبة
☐ تليفزيون	☐ ثلاجة
☐ كتاب	☑ كمبيوتر
☐ سيارة	☑ قلم
☐ تليفون	☑ مجلة
☑ مائدة	☑ كرسي

Page 37: Which word?

بجانب 5 ; على 4 ; فوق 3 ; تحت 2 ; أمام 1
في 8 ; وراء 7 ; تحت 6

ANSWERS

Page 39: Where are the mice
There are many possible sentences.
If you can, check yours with a native speaker.

Page 41: True or False?
1 True; 2 True; 3 True; 4 False; 5 True; 6 True; 7 False;
8 False; 9 False; 10 True

Topic 5

Page 44: Can you remember?
Check your answers with the Key Words panel on page 44.

Page 46: What does it mean?

قهوة صغيرة	(a) small coffee
صورة غالية	(an) expensive picture
كلب صغير	(a) small dog
كنبة جديدة	(a) new sofa
بيت صغير	(a) small house
سيارة قديمة جدا	(a) very old car
سندويتش كبير	(a) big sandwich
شجر طويل جدا	very tall trees

Page 47: Listen and check
1 False; 2 True; 3 True; 4 False; 5 True; 6 True; 7 False

Page 47: Unscramble the sentences
1 (reading the boxes left to right) c, a, b; 2 b, a, c;
3 c, a, d, b; 4 a, b, c, d

Page 50: Which word?
1 رأس ; 2 غريب ; 3 سمين ; 4 فم ; 5 ذيل ;
6 شعر ; 7 جميل ; 8 أنف ; 9 رفيع ; 10 قبيح

Page 51: At the pet show
هذه __6__ جميلة. ذيلها __4__ جدا و __1__ صغير وجميل.
__3__ الكلب قبيح وغريب. ذيله __5__ وانفه كبير __2__ !

Page 52: What does it look like?
There are many possible sentences.
If you can, check yours with a native speaker.

Topic 6

Page 55: Questions and answers

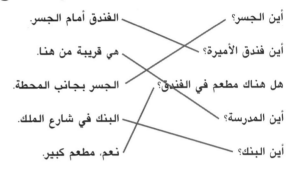

الفندق أمام الجسر. ——— أين الجسر؟
هي قريبة من هنا. ——— أين فندق الأميرة؟
الجسر بجانب المحطة. ——— هل هناك مطعم في الفندق؟
البنك في شارع الملك. ——— أين المدرسة؟
نعم، مطعم كبير. ——— أين البنك؟

Page 57: Word Square
car, boat, taxi,
airplane, bicycle,
bus, train

Page 60: Which way?
1. الحديقة من أين؟ خذ أول شارع على اليمين.
   al-Hadeeqa min ayna? книтн awwal shaari' 'ala l-yameen.
2. محطة الأتوبيس من أين؟ على طول.
   maHaTTat al-otobees min ayna? 'ala Tool.
3. الفندق من أين؟ خذ ثاني شارع على اليمين.
   al-funduq min ayna? книтн thaanee shaari' 'ala l-yameen.
4. البنك من أين؟ خذ ثاني شارع على اليسار.
   al-bank min ayna? книтн thaanee shaari' 'ala l-yameen.
5. المطار من أين؟ خذ القطار.
   al-maTaar min ayna? книтн al-qiTaar.
6. المتحف من أين؟ خذ الأتوبيس.
   al-matHaf min ayna? книтн al-otobees.

Page 61: Around town
These are model answers. Yours may vary slightly.
Karim Hotel
على طول وفندق كريم على اليمين.
'ala Tool wa funduq kareem 'ala l-yameen.

the park

على طول من هنا وبعد ذلك خذ أول شارع على اليسار. الحديقة بجانب المدرسة. 'ala Tool min huna wa ba'da THaalik khuTH awwal shaari' 'ala l-yasaar. al-Hadeeqa bi-jaanib al-madrasa.

the bus station

على طول من هنا وبعد ذلك خذ أول شارع على اليسار. محطة الأتوبيس على اليمين أمام المدرسة. 'ala Tool min huna wa ba'da THaalik khuTH awwal shaari' 'ala l-yasaar. maHattat al-otobees 'ala l-yameen amaam al-madrasa.

Page 62: Unscramble the conversation

e, b, c, a, g, d, f

Page 63: Game

Topic 7

Page 65: What does it mean?

Check your answers with the Key Words panel on page 64.

Page 67: Family Tree

Here are some possible sentences. Yours may vary.

زينة هي أم سارة. zayna hiya umm saara.

زينة هي أم يوسف. zayna hiya umm yoosef.

أحمد هو أبو سارة. aHmad huwa aboo saara.

أحمد هو أبو يوسف. aHmad huwa aboo yoosef.

سارة هي ابنة أحمد وزينة. saara hiya ibnat aHmad wa zayna.

يوسف هو ابن أحمد وزينة. yoosef huwa ibn aHmad wa zayna.

يوسف هو أخو سارة. yoosef huwa akhoo saara.

سارة هي أخت يوسف. saara hiya ukht yoosef.

أحمد هو زوج زينة. aHmad huwa zawj zayna.

Page 68: Family Tree

Page 68: Questions and answers

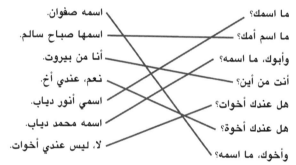

Page 71: How many?

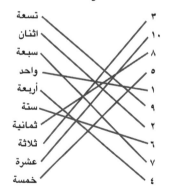

Page 71: Arabic sums

ثلاثة 5 ؛ ثمانية 4 ؛ ستة 3 ؛ أربعة 1 ؛
واحد 10 ؛ تسعة 9 ؛ عشرة 8 ؛ خمسة 7 ؛ تسعة 6

Topic 8

Page 75: What does it mean?
Check your answers with the Key Words panel on page 74.

Page 75: The tools of the trade

مهندس / مدرس / طبيب / محاسب / ممثل / سائق / طباخ

Page 77: Listen and note
1 *First name:* Mariam; *Family name:* al-Hajj; *Nationality:* Moroccan; *Spouse:* Mustafa; *Children:* 3; *Occupation:* doctor

2 *First name:* Salim; *Family name:* Osman; *Nationality:* Egyptian; *Spouse:* Manal; *Children:* 1; *Occupation:* chemistry teacher

Page 78: What does it mean?
a6, b5, c4, d1, e2, f3

Page 78: Which word?
اسمي هاري وأنا ____2____ . أنا من
ملبورن في ____4____ . زوجتي
____3____ جوسلين و ____5____ ابن
اسمه ____1____ .

Page 80: Word Square

أنا طباخ وأنا أعمل في مطعم.
ana Tabbaakh wa-ana a'mal fee maT'am.

أنا ممثل وأنا أعمل في مسرح.
ana mumaththil wa-ana a'mal fee masraH.

أنا مدرس وأنا أعمل في مدرسة.
ana mudarris wa-ana a'mal fee madrasa.

أنا صياد وأنا أعمل على مركب.
ana SayyaaD wa-ana a'mal 'ala markib.

أنا محاسب وأنا أعمل في بنك.
ana muHaasib wa-ana a'mal fee bank.

أنا موظف وأنا أعمل في مكتب.
ana muwaZZaf wa-ana a'mal fee maktab.

أنا طبيب وأنا أعمل في مستشفى.
ana Tabeeb wa-ana a'mal fee mustashfa.

Page 81: What are they saying?
1d, 2e, 3b, 4c, 5a, 6f

Page 82: Which word?
أنا علي ____7____ من دمشق في ____2____ . أنا أعمل ____3____
مدينة نيويورك. أنا ____8____ في ____5____ لبناني هناك. زوجتي مدرسة في
مدرسة ____1____ قريبة من المطعم. ____6____ ثلاث ____4____ : سارة، منى وفاطمة.

Test Yourself

Page 84: May I have...?
Use either. ممكن ... من فضلك. **mumkin ... min faDlak.** *or*
أريد ... من فضلك. **ureed ... min faDlak.** with the following:
١ فلافل ٢ كرسي ٣ سندويتش ٤ كولا ٥ قهوة ٦ فطيرة ٧ قلم ٨ كعكة

Page 85: Listen and check
1 True; 2 False; 3 True; 4 False; 5 False; 6 False

Page 85: Which word?
اسمي ____8____ . ____5____ من حلب، مدينة ____7____ في سوريا.
أنا مدرسة ____2____ السعودية و ____6____ طبيب هناك في ____1____
قريب ____4____ المدرسة. عندنا أربعة ____3____ : ابن وثلاث بنات.

Page 86: Read and check
1 True; 2 True; 3 False; 4 True; 5 False; 6 True; 7 True; 8 True; 9 False

Page 87: Read and check
children أطفال aTfaal		*brother* أخ akh	
husband زوج zawj		*daughters* بنات banaat	
sons أبناء abnaa'		*child* طفل Tifl	
daughter ابنة ibna		*wife* زوجة zawja	
father أب ab		*brothers* إخوة ikhwa	
mother أم umm		*son* ابن ibn	
sister أخت ukht		*sisters* أخوات akhawaat	

Page 87: How do you say it?
1. زوجي طبيب. **zawjee Tabeeb.**
2. عندي أربعة أطفال. **'indee arba'a aTfaal.**
3. ابنه مهندس. **ibnuh muhandis.**
4. أم سمير من السعودية. **umm sameer min as-sa'oodiyya.**
5. اسم زوجتي جوسلين. **ism zawjatee "Jocelyn".**
6. أخي ممثل. **akhee mumaththil.**
7. ليس عندي أخوات. **laysa 'indee akhawaat.**
8. عندي ثلاث بنات. **'indee thalaath banaat.**

Page 88: At the tourist office
أتوبيس	*bus*	مع السلامة	*goodbye*
قريب	*near*	شكرا	*thank you*
كبير	*big*	وراء	*behind*
متحف	*museum*	على اليمين	*on the right*
أين	*where*	على اليسار	*on the left*
صباح الخير	*good morning*	شارع	*street*

Name cards:

✂

سمير	يوسف	زينة	فاطمة
تشازلز	بيتار	هاري	ماري
مارك	نانسي	جاين	سام
لوسي	توني	سوزان	بيني

Sentence-build cards:

✂

؟	(أنا) اسمي	الأستاذ	صباح
.	الآنسة	شكرا	الخير
يا	اسمك	من فضلك	مساء
ما	مدام	مع سلامة	أهلا

Fatima	Zayna	Yoosef	Sameer
Mary	Harry	Peter	Charles
Sam	Jane	Nancy	Mark
Penny	Suzanne	Tony	Lucy

morning	Mr.	my name is	?
good	thank you	Miss	.
evening	please	your name	
hello	goodbye	Mrs.	what's

Picture cards:

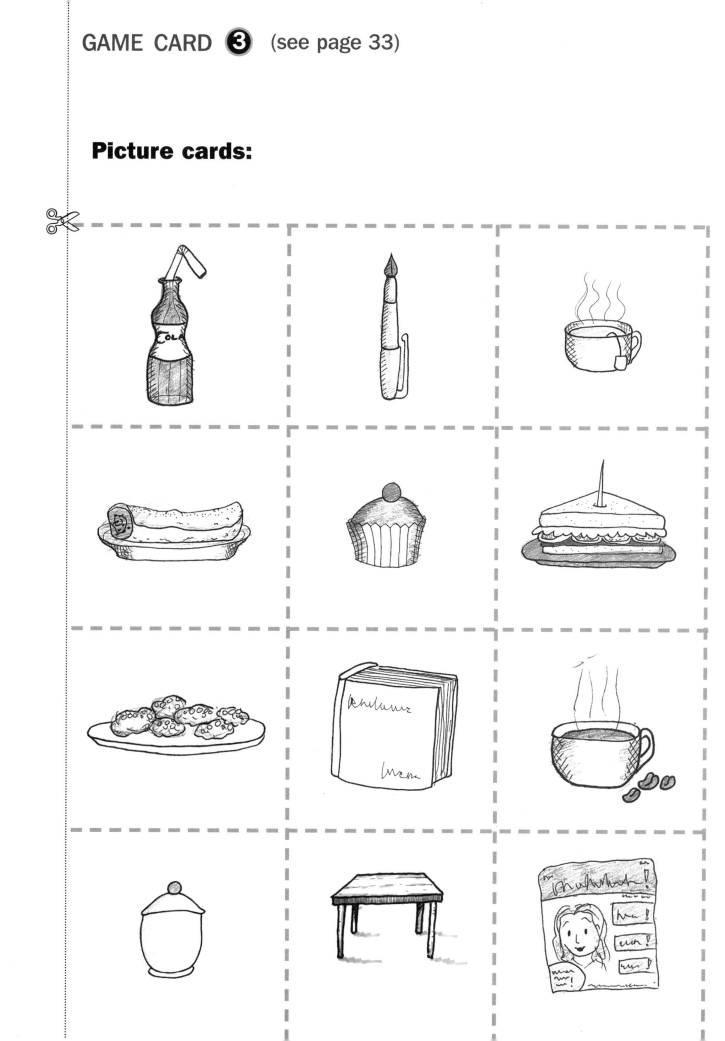

Cut-out pictures (cut round small pictures)

Sentence-build cards:

في	على	تحت	فوق
تليفزيون	بجانب	وراء	أمام
.	و	هناك	ليس هناك
الغرفة	الشباك	المائدة	الكرسي
سندويتش	صورة	تليفون	السرير
قطة	كلب	فأر	كمبيوتر

above	under	on	in
in front of	behind	next to	a television
there isn't	there is	and	.
the chair	the table	the window	the room
the bed	a telephone	a picture	a sandwich
a computer	a mouse	a dog	a cat

Picture cards:

Adjective cards:

جديد	طويل	قبيح	غريب
قديم	صغير	قصير	سمين
جميل	كبير	غالٍ	رخيص

Picture cards:

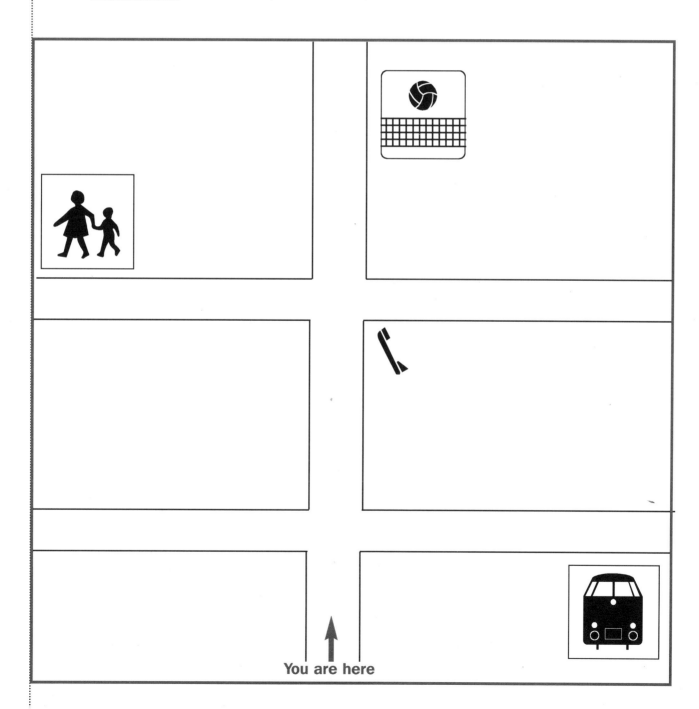

You are here

GAME CARD ❼ (see page 73)

٤	١	٧	٩
١٠	٨	٣	٢
٥	٦	٧	١
٦	٩	٤	٦

٢	١٠	٣	١
٨	٥	٦	٧
٥	٨	١٠	٩
٣	٤	٧	٣

١
٢
٣
٤
٥
٦
٧
٨
٩
١٠

Picture cards:

Profession cards:

محاسب	سائق	طبيب	طباخ
صياد	طالب	ممثل	موظف
مدرس	مهندس		